POLICING AND
COIN OPERATIONS

Published by Books Express Publishing
Copyright © Books Express, 2011
ISBN 978-1-780399-23-2

Books Express publications are available from all good retail and online booksellers. For
publishing proposals and direct ordering please contact us at: info@books-express.com

POLICING AND COIN OPERATIONS:
LESSONS LEARNED, STRATEGIES, AND FUTURE DIRECTIONS

Samuel Musa, John Morgan, and Matt Keegan

2011

Contents

Preface

The idea for this monograph was started in early January 2010 with the initial concept to conduct research on predictive policing and write a paper on the subject. After several meetings and many ideas considered for the paper, the co-editors realized that there is a need to expand the target to the role of policing in counterinsurgency. This was a hot topic and there were many diverse views in the literature on what the role should be. As the ideas on this new direction began to materialize, it became clear that this was a monumental task that would require a workshop to gather and exchange ideas from a diverse group of experts. The group then began to consider the framework for the workshop and the desired outcome to influence policymakers on the future directions of the role of policing. Several options were then considered on how to go about achieving this goal. The idea of a monograph then emerged as a good starting point.

The concept of having multiple sessions with each moderator writing a chapter summarizing their session coupled with their ideas on the subject began to evolve. Selecting the moderators and the speakers and restricting the attendance to those invited guests became the next task. The workshop was then held on September 29, 2010, as a co-sponsored event by the Center for Technology and National Security Policy (CTNSP) of the National Defense University (NDU) and the Combating Terrorism Technical Support Office (CTTSO) of the Threat Support Working Group (TSWG) of the Department of Defense. The workshop was focused on lessons learned from past campaigns, development of new strategies, and outlining future directions for implementation. Participants included leading authors on the subject, selected individuals from Defense, Justice, and State Departments, Law Enforcement, Service Academies, and Training Commands and Think Tanks. Also, select National War College (NWC) and Industrial College of Armed Forces (ICAF) students with recent experience in Iraq/Afghanistan participated in the workshop. It was a real success based on the feedback from the participants. Many of the new ideas generated are presented in this monograph.

The authors would like to take this opportunity to thank the speakers, moderators, and co-sponsoring organizations. The authors gratefully acknowledge the financial support of Starnes Walker, former Director of Research, and Matt Clark, Director of University Programs, Science and Technology Directorate, Department of Homeland Security. The authors also thank Samuel Bendett, Research Associate at CTNSP, for his extensive support and for providing organizational, logistical, and editorial assistance.

This effort could not have been produced without Ted Woodcock, who was the editor for this project. His contributions, support, and dedication to this effort are greatly appreciated. The authors are also very grateful to Elizabeth Woodcock for the cover design of this monograph.

ഌ

The views expressed in this monograph are those of the authors and the contributors to the chapters and do not reflect the official policy or position of the National Defense University, the Combating Terrorism Technical Support Office, the Department of Defense, or the U.S. Government. All information and sources for this monograph were drawn from unclassified materials.

Chapter 1: Introduction to Policing and COIN Operations

Samuel Musa, John Morgan, and Matt Keegan

INTRODUCTION

At the time of this writing, the United States and the other members of the International Security Assistance Forces are completing nearly a decade of conflict in Iraq and Afghanistan. What started as more conventional or traditional fights has degenerated over time into insurgency warfare, something U.S. Forces have had to re-learn and re-build to fight. Re-learn and re-build are key elements as U.S. Forces have fought insurgencies in the past, but consistently maintained forces to fight more conventional warfare. Counterinsurgency (COIN) is very different from armored vehicles rolling through the Fulda Gap, or the race to Baghdad. It is a fight not against a Government as much as it is a fight for control of the mind-set of the population by non-state actors in a race to gain popular support. It is a grassroots battle that not only requires military force, but security established at the local level through everyday police presence that represents the Rule of Law, the national Government, and safety and stability locally. It is against this backdrop that the Center for Technology and National Security Policy (CTNSP) and the Combating Terrorism Technical Support Office (CTTSO) came together to look at Policing and COIN and the ways, methods, and techniques that could be shared to help overcome the insurgencies Coalition forces face. The efforts of the CTNSP at the National Defense University (NDU) and the CTTSO culminated in a one-day workshop held on September 29, 2010, on Policing and COIN Operations: Lessons Learned, Strategies, and Future Directions.

It is important to understand who these organizations are in order to establish the value of the contribution. CTNSP combines scientific and technical assessments with analyses of current strategic and defense policy issues, taking on topics to bridge the gap. The Center has produced studies on proliferation and homeland security, military transformation, international science and technology, information technology, life sciences, and social science modeling, and provides technical and policy expertise to the faculty and students at the National Defense University. CTTSO fields rapid combating terrorism solutions to meet continually evolving requirements defined by end users. Working closely with over 100 Government agencies, State, and local government, law enforcement organizations, and national first responders, CTTSO leverages technical expertise, operational objectives, and interagency sponsor funding. CTTSO operates as a program office under the Assistant Secretary of Defense (ASD) for Special Operations and Low-Intensity Conflict and Interdependent Capabilities (SO/LIC & IC). Together these two organizations combine the "policy with the practical" and through the workshop opened new discussions on knowledge sharing that can contribute to enabling the COIN war fighter to better accomplish the mission.

The workshop was focused on lessons learned from past campaigns, development of new strategies and outlining future directions for implementation. Participants included leading authors on the subject, selected individuals from Defense, Justice and State Departments, Law Enforcement, Service Academies, and Training Commands and Think Tanks. Also, select National War College (NDU) and Industrial College of Armed Forces (NDU) students with recent experience in Iraq/Afghanistan participated in the workshop. Together, the many panelists offered recent real-world experience in this multi-layered issue of addressing COIN and maintaining/returning stability to nations facing insurgency threats.

As stated earlier, the current conflicts are not the first time the U.S. military has been faced with COIN, but seemingly is re-learning lessons of the past. In thinking, methods, processes and procedures can be institutionalized. Then, when this threat faces the U.S. again, we may be able to shorten the magnitude and duration of such conflict. Not only should these military lessons be institutionalized, but they must be open to encompass solutions from across the spectrum of COIN, ranging from high intensity military operations to day-to-day stability actions at the policing level . . . something traditionally not considered by a "conventional war fighting" machine. To that end, the American military, when confronted with irregular warfare actions, should leverage proven methods developed not only in prior military solutions to COIN, but in policing to interdict insurgent or terrorist activity and enhance legitimacy of friendly governments through extension of the Rule of Law. It is well known that the military has strength in COIN operations, counterterrorism, and special operations. Concurrently, the police have strength in border control and civilian authority in stability of operations. Relevant policing techniques include identity-fixing, forensic evidence collection, real-time situational awareness, and community engagement. When applied broadly and consistently, these approaches multiply the effectiveness of military forces and build the governance capacity of host countries.

Many important approaches are being tried by the military that align with policing tactics. What is missing is a strategic approach that uses these tactics as a core element of COIN. Further, it is critical that indigenous police forces learn to use these techniques to maintain security and improve legitimacy. Properly applied, policing techniques have transformed American cities while greatly improving the regard that communities have for the police. LAPD is a good example. Of course, if used improperly or with too heavy a hand, police-type techniques may be counter-productive. They could make foreign forces seem too intrusive or as an occupying force. That's why the partnership with capable, local forces and community engagement are critical, in addition to technological approaches. In order to set the stage for the topics to be covered in this monograph, a brief introduction to the fundamental assumptions surrounding policing and counterinsurgency operations will be addressed here.

FUNDAMENTAL ASSUMPTIONS

Insurgency warfare is again proving to be a battle with no discernable "front lines." Combatants frequently have no uniforms and don't fight according to conventional tenants. They use the population as their hiding place, which can allow them to appear suddenly, strike, and disappear back into the crowd. This makes it extremely difficult to pick the good guy out from the bad guy and to do this "picking" in a timely fashion permitting actionable information to be gathered and disseminated. This points to a main problem: that of providing information relevant to the "human terrain" in which COIN operations are executed. The military/intelligence community has the resources to provide actionable intelligence based on the extensive resources available but may not have the local knowledge or relationships necessary to gain timely ground truth. Conversely, the police can provide information based on trust/legitimacy. In order to understand how these communities interact with each other, it is necessary to start with the fundamental assumptions relating to policing operations. The basic applications of policing are:

1. Use of policing techniques in military operations.
   a. COIN.
   b. Special operations other than war.
   c. Traditional symmetric warfare.
   d. Border control.

2. Building rule of law within a chaotic area.
   a. Military-Policing combined operations.
   b. AFP International Deployment Group/ICITAP activities, which will be discussed later in the monograph.
   c. The role of existing institutions (central, tribal, NGO, etc.).

3.   The influence of military operations on American policing.
     a.   Tactical operations, communications, field forensics.
     b.   Professional structures (e.g., hierarchical command).

The key issues are when does the military operation end and the policing operation start? What is then done in the middle of this transition, and how is such a transition executed? How does this transition return the Rule of Law?

As the leading world power, America is interested in extending the Rule of Law in unstable areas. This extension allows the following; it promotes international stability (assuming that stability will lead in the long term to outcomes in the American national interest, which assumes continuing American hegemony). It also prevents the spread of terrorism and transnational crime, and it enables the expansion of commerce. In addition, it creates the conditions for democratic evolution and development. It then follows that "develop nation" conceptions of policing and the Rule of Law will be welcomed and beneficial in unstable areas. This allows conflicts with local values to be resolved (e.g., Sharia law).

Everyone wants to have a sense of safety and security for their family and community. The responsiveness and capability of policing functions are the bases for the legitimacy of any state.

There is a conflict between policing functions and federal/military functions. The military should not be expected to perform policing functions or to build Rule of Law in general. The military can support these efforts, but a commitment from non-DOD partners is essential. There are *Posse Comitatus* concerns as well as operational concerns that undermine military philosophy. Furthermore, the federal government should not be expected to perform traditional policing functions inside the United States, which are the responsibility of state and local governments. Next, let us consider the police methods and COIN.

POLICE METHODS AND COIN

There are a number of police methods to counter crime that may be applicable to counterinsurgency. These are described below:

1.   Counterinsurgency and policing have common elements.
     a.   In saying this, we recognize that military operations are fundamentally different from policing operations. Military units can benefit from tactics that have been successful in

      policing, but these tactics must be adapted to the context of military engagement.

  b. Engagement with local populations is much more common than engagement with enemy combatants.

     i. Legitimacy is a critical measure of success for both.

     ii. Understanding of the specific community is critical for success because it permits the leveraging of local community leaders.

  c. The soldier and police officer encounter many more situations with risk, but generally much lower risk than in active combat.

     i. Management of risk is therefore critical. Generally, because force is asymmetric, time is on the side of the cop and the soldier in a particular incident, which can be used to mitigate risk.

     ii. Force protection needs to be oriented to the mobile individual or unit. Body armor is more important than walls. Protection of static facilities is about good sensor information around the facility to detect threats.

  d. Intelligence is often more important than the ability to project force.

     i. Every incident is an opportunity to gain knowledge that may not provide intelligence specific to the incident itself but may be valuable in a larger context.

  e. When force is needed, it is generally very directed and specific, with limited objectives.

     i. Use of force is not necessarily intended to be lethal on the target (almost never in LE), so training/doctrine/kit needs to reflect that intention.

  f. Breaches of residential and commercial buildings are more common than defeat of fortified positions.

2. Insurgency and organized crime have common elements.

  a. Both often rely on illicit activity to provide money.

     i. Financial flows are critical paths.

     ii. Drug markets, counterfeiting, smuggling, gambling, prostitution, identity theft: these are money-makers for organized crime. How about insurgents?

b. Recruitment/retention/desistance.
    i. Insurgent groups follow tribal/family/religious/community loyalties, much like organized crime.
        1. Organized crime is opportunity-based. Like-minded criminals work together for common interests for a time, but that may not last if those interests collide. Is insurgency similar in that respect?
    ii. Insurgent recruitment may be dependent on economic incentives. Although this has been argued for crime, it is seldom true today. Criminal activity is more about social problems like missing fathers and misogynistic culture.

3. Police have developed tactics to deal with crime that may be useful to counter-insurgency.
    a. Identity-fixing and biometrics.
        i. Biometric identification has a long history in policing for multiple applications, including offender tracking (is this the right prisoner?), identification of presence at a crime scene (e.g., latent print analysis), and access control. Each of these has a COIN analog.
    b. Forensic evidence.
        i. Forensic evidence is used to establish the perpetrator and develop the evidence of how the individual did a crime. The latter is just as important for criminal justice as the former, because the mere presence of DNA or latent prints do not establish the guilt of the individual. Multiple techniques are relevant to these two objectives in COIN. Some examples:
           1. DNA analysis.
               a. Bodily fluids are often left at crime scenes, including blood, semen, saliva.
               b. Trace DNA may be present in a variety of places, including shattered glass, cigarettes/food items, fingerprints, etc.

        c. DNA can be used to source an individual apart from STR-matching of identity, e.g., in COIN for tribal identification.

    2. Impression evidence, including latent prints, tire/shoe marks, etc.

    3. Trace evidence.

        a. Chemical residue: to identify individuals who have used a firearm or worked in bomb-making.

        b. Other types of residue.

It is clear from the above key elements that there are many policing methods applicable to COIN. The next step is to identify the information relevant to the human terrain and the situational awareness of this "human topography." These are the issues for dealing with situational awareness.

SITUATIONAL AWARENESS

There are a number of factors that have impact on situational awareness. These are listed below.

1. Common operating picture: Units share basic information concerning identities and activities of insurgent or friendly groups and individuals (or those of unknown loyalty) on a constant basis. There is a basic understanding of the big picture of operations in the region around an AO.

2. Community understanding: Units understand the nature and history (recent history especially) of key groups and leaders in their AO. They understand the economics and culture of towns and neighborhoods well enough to detect anomalies.

3. Patrol awareness: Individual soldiers have awareness of their areas of patrol. Patrol occurs using the least intrusive level of protection possible (i.e., on foot) but with the greatest degree of engagement possible (i.e., directly with as broad a cross-section of individuals, businesses, and institutions as possible). This provides daily situational awareness to improve the identification of criminal or insurgent behavior, individuals who "don't belong," and vehicles/structures/goods that may be associated with insurgent activity.

4. Geospatial analysis: This should not be underestimated. Police have used geospatial analysis to allocate and direct patrols, predict crime series, guide city planning, and achieve other objectives, for a long time. Geospatial analysis may be the one area where COIN has progressed furthest to learn from law enforcement.

Community policing has taken many forms in policing, but all of them start with the concept that crime can be prevented through community engagement and non-kinetic force. Elements include the following:

1. Neighborhood development, including the design of public spaces to promote use by citizens and limit opportunities for criminal activity (e.g., Biederman rules, lighting, etc.).

2. Neighborhood-level   engagement: Everything   from neighborhood watch groups to community leader engagement strategies to Project DARE are followed by community police officers who are dedicated to these purposes. Are there individuals within COIN operations who are analogous?

3. Engagement: Two new approaches have each been called Ceasefire, but they share the goal of directly engaging offenders and their families and communities to promote their desistance from crime. The idea is to provide a culture of abiding by the law and contributing to society. (As an aside, the most effective way to get someone to go "straight" is to either age them out of crime or get them married or with a long-term girlfriend.)

Police depend on superior situational awareness within the local level of the human terrain every day. Conversely, conventionally trained military units are trained to fight based on military intelligence and not the sort of "cop on the beat" intelligence police live by. In COIN, where maneuver warfare of heavy forces has a minimal role at best, the military could certainly take the lessons learned by the police and test them against the COIN mission.

In order to have a better understanding of the relationship between policing and COIN, it is critical that we examine some of the lessons learned from previous conflicts in this introduction. These are summarized in the following section.

EXAMPLES OF LESSONS LEARNED

In the following chapters, lessons learned from a number of past and current operations are explored. These are based on the specific experience of the speakers, particularly in the Iraq and Afghanistan theaters of operations. In this section, we cite a few examples based on the open literature as a matter of introduction.

OPERATION BLUE STAR (INDIA, 1984)

Operation Blue Star, which took place in June 1984, was an Indian military operation ordered by Indira Ghandi, Prime Minister of India, to remove Sikh separatists from the Golden Temple in Amritsar. The separatists, led by Singh Bhindranwale, were accused of amassing weapons in the temple. The operation was carried out by Indian army troops. Although it was militarily successful, the operation aroused immense controversy, and the government's justification for the timing and style of the attack are highly debated. Some of the issues surrounding this operation are as follows:

1. A state cannot wait until the insurgents create an enclave/separate area of operations from which they can strike or conduct their policies. Some of the complaints about Operation Blue Star were that the situation should not have been allowed to get to that point to begin with.

2. If the insurgents/guerrillas/fighters pose a non-negotiable threat, specific direct policies should be put in place against them early on—whether such policy is capture, neutralization, or expulsion from the state proper.

3. In the case of religion-backed/inspired insurgency, the state should promote moderate/non-violent leaders from the community in question so as to create a powerful counterweight to more extreme viewpoints. By the time India chose to act forcefully, Singh Bhindranwale was already considered a sacred guru whose non-compromising stance on Sikh issues was a call to action.

4. The state must make intelligence on weapons trafficking/acquisition one of its top priorities when dealing with religion-backed/inspired anti-state movements and formations.

5. The state should be aware if any foreign assistance is given to the insurgents/guerrilla fighters. In this case, the Indian military was concerned that Pakistan may be supporting Bhindranwale's movement for an independent Sikh state.

6. Actionable intelligence on the specific target is key, especially if it is known that civilians as well as militants are going to be congregating in the target area. Indian military overestimated the rebels' strength and used overwhelming force.

7. Attempt peaceful negotiations firsthand, if only to find out the intent and purpose of the insurgents/guerrilla's actions. Armed action should be the choice of the last resort.

8. If possible, an attack against the insurgents/guerrillas should not be carried out on a day that is holy or scared for the religion of the other side—such an attack shows disrespect and disregard of the religious and social norms of the other party. Indian military chose to attack the Golden Temple on the holiest day for the Sikhs worldwide.

9. A state must remember and recognize the contribution made by a specific ethno-religious community to the nation—Sikhs were some of the most active supporters of India's independence from Great Britain, and formed a significant portion of its nascent armed forces. Such respect can be a powerful reconciling tool if/when the conflict has reached the armed struggle stage.

10. Private or state media should be discouraged from openly taking sides in the conflict.

INDIAN STATE (http://panthic.org/articles/3332)

At the end of it all, two questions are asked by the Sikhs of Punjab. Was the Army action necessary and unavoidable? Secondly, if unavoidable, could it not have taken a different form, avoiding all the destruction and the bloodshed and the brutalities? Kirpal Singh, President of Khalsa Dewan, Amritsar, stated that "if the government had been sincere in its efforts in solving the Punjab problem, it would have solved it long ago even before the Blue Star Operation, and there would have been no cause for the Akalis and others to organize Morchas of the thousands of the people, from time to time, and the extremists would have been isolated and it would have become known as to who were the extremists, what kind of men they were, and what they had been doing. The Government could have negotiated with them. If the Government could talk with Laldenga of Mizos and extremists of the Nagaland, who had been fighting with our military for the last 31 years, then what was the difficulty in talking to the extremists of Punjab and asking them what they wanted, what they were fighting and why they were collecting arms?"

Similarly, S.S. Bhagowalia, who is the Vice-President of the Association for Protection of Democratic Rights (Punjab), was extremely forthright, "when the government in 1948 could control and capture Hyderbad from the Nizam who wanted to secede from independent India without any violence and killing of the common people, why this Government could not capture Bhindranwale with tact, without any damage to the Golden Temple? This has created tension and anger amongst the minds of the people." Surinder Singh Ragi gave another example—"The Indian Army had captured 93,000 soldiers of Pakistan army in Bangladesh in 1971 without bloodshed. Was bloodshed absolutely necessary at the Golden Temple to flush out a hundred or so terrorists?"

Hazara Singh Vadale, an employee of the SGPC, echoed a common sentiment: "The way the government of independent country attacked the Golden Temple reminded us of the medieval time when our religion was attacked and we are persecuted. Thousands of women, children, pilgrims, had gathered here on June 3 for Gurupurab. They had no connection with politics, why they shot down?"

Kirpal Singh, elaborating on the excesses committed said, "At the time of Blue Star Act, it could be known how many died of those who were fighting with the military but the fact is that due to Guru Purab Day hundreds of pilgrims had come and were staying in the premises of the Darbar Sahib. There were children and women among them. These pilgrims were unarmed and the military attacked them and killed them. Thereafter the military did not allow their dead bodies to be cremated by the relative nor handed over the same to them. Their dead bodies were insulted. No effort was made to record their names and addresses. Now it has created a lot of problem. For example, if any deceased has any insurance or bank balance or any land dispute, his heirs require death certificate but in absence of any record of it, they did not get any compensation. Even in the history of military wars, the people are allowed to take the dead bodies from each others' territories by showing white flags. When General Dyer killed people in Jallianwala Bagh, he also allowed the dead bodies to be taken by the relatives."

Shiv Singh Khushpuri, 65 years, a member of the S.G.P.C. from Gurdaspur district, said, "It was the duty of the State to identify the bodies of those who died in Operation Blue Star. After the Jallianwala Bagh massacre, the British Government identified those killed, handed over their bodies to the next kin and paid Rs. 2000 as compensation for every person killed in the incident. Whereas in Operation Blue Star, the present government of an apparently independent country has not only not identified those killed or missing, rather they are harassing and persecuting the families and friends of those who are reportedly missing."

S.S. Bhagowalia throws light on the efforts of the Government to suppress information. "The doctors who conducted the post-mortem of the victims of the army action at Golden Temple were simply terrorized. If there were 20 bullets in a body, they were forced to record only two bullet wounds, under the threat of being shot." This only indicates the extent of the massacre that took place and the ferocity with which the Army undertook the operation. The common feeling in Punjab is that it was indeed not an Operation against Bhindranwale and other so-called terrorists, according to the Government; it was an attack on the Sikhs "to teach them a lesson" so they would never again raise their heads or voices in protest.

Next, let us consider some of the lessons learned from Afghanistan. More detailed lessons from former theater commanders will be covered later in Chapter 5.

AFGHANISTAN (2001–PRESENT)

The ability of American forces to take and hold cities and villages in Afghanistan is severely limited by the ability of the central Afghan government to provide military and police resources in many parts of the country. In particular, insurgent strongholds are by their nature the least likely places for the Afghan government to provide effective security. Security, in this sense, is a political objective. A self-sustaining, legitimate government should be able to police neighborhoods and provide basic services, thus enabling the conditions for public support. Any situation in which American military assets provide the most visible security is by its nature an unstable situation, even if the dominance of American forces is meant to be temporary. Further, sustained foreign presence has been most successful where it is least needed, such as in Tajik or other areas not conducive to Taliban influence. In critical areas, the American military has been successful for a period of time, but these gains are undermined by several factors, including the lack of Afghan follow-up to take over security responsibilities, lack of legitimate government capacity, turnover in American military personnel, and the inability of foreign military forces to provide police services unrelated to force protection.

A relevant example is a mounted American military expedition traveling about an hour from its base to provide periodic medical services to a village. Insurgents were seen to observe the situation but not interfere. Such an operation does not change the fundamental security picture in the village or region and increases the vulnerability of American troops. It has humanitarian benefits, but even these are short-lived, because there is very little "leave-behind" building of indigenous capacity.

There are several media accounts of Afghan elders complaining about the turnover in American military liaisons. Successive commanders are informed by the local Afghan leader about their needs and security situation, often at great risk from retaliation. The American commander is replaced in eight months to a year, and the local commander must start over with a new person. They never see their counterpart ever again. The prototypical story is One Tribe at a Time, describing the successful liaison of a military unit with a tribe along the Afghan-Waziristan border. The relationship became so close and fruitful that the unit received intelligence about insurgent attacks from the tribe. Unfortunately, the story ends with the American soldier returning home, with a new unit and commander without a trusted relationship coming into the area. Past successful COIN campaigns assumed that the foreign power could not afford to rotate troops on an annual basis, so extended tours led to a force that was intimately familiar with the tribes, leadership, and relationships on the ground. The attempt by American forces to substitute intelligence analysis or "human terrain" analysis for this knowledge base is not sufficient.

Alternatively, there have been attempts to transform military forces using policing methods. Cop on the Beat and Combat Hunter are two programs used by the Marine Corps to train soldiers in the art of traditional police methods. These efforts emphasize the development of intelligence through engagement with local communities and situational awareness on patrol. The programs have been highly effective when employed. Cop on the Beat is now limited to only military police units within the Marine Corps, thus limiting the effectiveness of the training for COIN operators, who are not in MP units. Further, the programs contradict traditional military doctrine. Soldiers are not cops, follow very different rules of engagement and authority, and usually avoid non-kinetic contact and methods.

Thus, counterinsurgency operations are largely dependent on the capacity of Afghan army and police. Alternatively, the military may engage local tribal leaders to provide this capacity, but this option is limited by the weakness of Afghan tribes, which have been under siege for over 30 years, and the influence of the drug trade, which has also undermined traditional tribal loyalties and precepts. Further, reliance on local tribal forces undermines the central government even further, thus preventing the spread of the rule of law and the strengthening of the security forces essential to further gains.

Unfortunately, the Afghan army is not capable of sustained, independent actions and the Afghan police are extremely weak or corrupt. Thus, the counterinsurgency is often denied basic intelligence of the type that would be obtained by police and that would enable effective COIN. There will always be a "security gap" after the military gains control and before local police forces can become effective. In Afghanistan, the military is—for the most part—incapable of providing enough local security to substitute for local police in sufficient quantity and for a long enough period to prevent insurgent attacks and maintain local security. Even soldiers trained in COIN or Cop on the Beat–like methods cannot be expected to provide legitimacy for a government that does not show effective security on its own. They may—in ideal circumstances—perform some functions usually associated with stability police units (similar to gendarmerie) or border police, but they cannot respond to citizen calls for assistance, investigate crimes, or perform useful crowd control.

In particular, the situation in Afghanistan mirrors experience with wider violence, such as terrorist groups. In terrorism, groups form a continuum of methods from legitimate expression through extreme violence. In the same way, insurgent groups and tribes in Afghanistan form a continuum in which some are very loyal to the Karzai government, others oppose the government through democratic means, some maintain independent governance without violence, some engage in opportunistic violence based on local conditions or the drug trade, some seek autonomy through consistent, violent opposition, and some are ideologically committed to a violent overthrow of the central government. Only this last group can be considered implacably opposed to the central government and not susceptible to improvements in legitimacy through COIN operations. Also, very few of these various groups are best engaged through COIN as employed by the military without an effective, national civil police authority.

THE FOLLOWING CHAPTERS

This book is organized into several topics based on the workshop. First, Policy considerations from the Department of Defense and Department of Homeland Security are outlined in the Second Chapter. These are based on the perspectives of senior officials from these departments who have a major policy role. In the Third Chapter, we set the stage with two different approaches to the conflicts of policing and counterinsurgency. These are based on the visions of two prominent authors in this subject. In the Fourth Chapter, we cover the strategic lessons from American policing. We were fortunate to have leading representatives from the major police departments in the United States. They highlighted their experiences and perspectives on the fundamentals of American policing and the methods available to conduct counterterrorism operations. In the Fifth Chapter, CTNSP and CTTSO were pleased to have students from both the National War College and the Industrial College of the Armed Forces who have recently returned from theater operations. They provided us with the lessons learned from Iraq/Afghanistan operations.

In the Sixth Chapter, we go back in recent history and highlight some of the lessons learned in past conflicts. These observations were based on actual experiences of the speakers, complemented by interviews of other recent COIN war fighters. In the Seventh Chapter, we consider the fundamental issues of COIN policy and process. These thoughts were based on in-depth studies conducted by the speakers and published in leading Journals. In the Eighth Chapter, we consider the fundamental issues in building an indigenous policing capacity. The examples presented were a result of specific programs in existence such as the Australian International Deployment Group and others in-depth.

At the completion of reading these pages, the authors hope that the reader walks away armed with increased knowledge of policing and COIN parallels and is now able to ask better questions about how America can be better prepared to bring such conflicts to a successful conclusion. The answers to the many questions may not lie in these pages, but the information necessary to start the search for the answers does. Whether the answers are here in black and white, or the path to answers begins within these pages, this monograph establishes an attempt to document lessons learned in policing and COIN and will hopefully start a trend of retaining such lessons so American forces are better prepared and do not have to relearn what they have learned before.

Chapter 2: Policy Considerations—The Department of Defense and Department of Homeland Security

THE DEPARTMENT OF DEFENSE

James Schear

Deputy Assistant Secretary of Defense for
Partnership Strategy and Stability Operations,
United States Department of Defense

Indigenous police success is a key ingredient in the success or failure of the counterinsurgency (COIN) mission. Police are an integral part of the stabilization landscape. Police are part of the landscape but the character of their presence is diverse—including monitoring, enforcing, training, and advising. There are many examples: Kosovo, Israel, and others. What can we say about these experiences? I am eager to learn from you. I would like to provoke discussion and feedback on the following assertions.

1. Indigenous policing is absolutely vital to the overall success of the counterinsurgency mission. Police with contacts to the local communities will perform better than extended military units who may not be attuned to the local needs. However, corruption of the police is a problem and can create severe obstacles to progress. You have probably heard of the story of how Afghan farmers get stopped by police 8 times and are shaken down so badly they have no money left over to buy produce for themselves.

2. Pre-war police traditions are not all alike—there are dangers at over-generalizing. Somalian, Haitian, and Bosnian police have different degrees of politicization in their ranks. One should be careful at overgeneralizing at the nature of the baseline. An appropriate precaution would appear to be to withhold judgment until one is actually deployed on the ground.

3. In police business, gaining physical access is hard, but achieving cognitive access—which involves figuring out how people operate, how they react to your presence—is much harder.

4. Local supply of police trainers and advisers is chronically short compared to the demand. Looking all over the world at COIN operations—and beyond COIN—a lot of the missions are looking like the police missions. In Haiti, I don't see any mission for the military other than a police mission. However exceptions to the rule exist—Brazilian military units patrolling the slums, working with the local police, is an example of a role for military forces within COIN operations. Available resources must be used in the best possible way since the supply and demand for police forces is a chronic problem.

5. There is a competing demand between achieving quick impact on the one hand and sustainability on the other. As an example, in the case of the Anbar province in Iraq: while the training for the Sons of Iraq movement was undertaken quickly, the real challenge was to achieve sustainability for the force over a longer timeframe.

6. The police component is just one part of an overall package that also must include corrections, the courts, and other systems. How to achieve balanced development and integrated deployment and use of law enforcement, judicial, correctional, and other related assets in diverse types of mission is still under discussion.

7. In sustainability projects, tensions exist between the need to conduct police reform on the national level and the coordinated undertaking of such reforms on the local level. In some countries, the population diversity is such that the national police units tend to look like occupiers when deployed locally. However if the police force is formed and deployed from purely local personnel, familiarity may increase the likelihood of corruption.

8. Washington-level challenge: The United States is not well structured to be a good player here—DoD and State each have some capacities that sometimes work. That's a legal authority's funding challenge. There are new and better ways that we should be able to structure ourselves. We would like to keep the security forces' police capacity front and center as we look at this problem.

9. We should not overlook some positive cases, especially in the Palestinian Authority efforts over the past few efforts (granted, it is an unusual case on the local level).

QUESTIONS AND DISCUSSION

Discussion involved questions related to security assistance, expanding civilian capacity, and the development of internationally deployable police assets.

*   *Security Assistance:* We are committed to the Presidential Policy Directive that will address the basic principles and practices in security assistance management. In broad terms, the stakeholders in the community are more diverse than previously imagined: The Department of State, INL, DHS, counternarcotics agencies, and OSD. There is an argument that the current patchwork system is better suited to what we need. I would highlight that there is a high likelihood that we will try to unveil a new system—a concept of shared responsibility that works across a large spectrum of training, equipment, and ministerial capacity. There may be a very focused piece of that with regard to the rule of law and capacity-building in areas where the civilian providers are challenged.

*   *Expanding Civilian Capacity:* The questioner suggested that there never has been political will to have excess capacity in police the way we have excess capacity with the military strength. It was observed that excess military capacity does not get you off the hook when figuring out the scaling and the ground situation. In Haiti, after the recent earthquake, the number of U.S. troops deployed in that country was increased from several hundred boots on the ground to over 20,000. If the U.S. had more access to appropriate types of civilian expertise, it would be possible to get the best out of our military in terms of the types of performance in the civilian area and achieve more sustainable results. It would be nice to have someone on the team who knows the human terrain, to have the civil-military presence, and Afghanistan is probably a laboratory for that. To focus on the complexity of the overall problem, yesterday, at the Global Leadership Conference, Secretaries Clinton, Gates, Geithner, and the USAID Administrator were talking about global development with a focus on how to rebuild the capabilities of USAID.

- *Internationally-Deployable Police:* It was observed that the Australian International Police are capable of deploying police forces internationally in a rapid and efficient manner and that the U.S. does not have the structure to create a similar organization. A question was asked whether there was any interest or effort to develop a surge capacity in the U.S. in order to undertake policing. It was observed that developing the right formula to work that would involve input from the Justice and State Department authorities, and funding to build that capacity would be helpful. There are people in both Departments that share a desire to move in that direction, but it is very hard. They would have to work it out. Furthermore, it was observed that the biggest difference between the U.S. and Australia in terms of providing support for international policing activities was that Australia has one clear agency in charge of police, while the United States has at least a thousand agencies. Every country organizes its law enforcement differently. There are 1,000 officers and their support staff in the Australian force, for example.

THE DEPARTMENT OF HOMELAND SECURITY

Arif Alikhan

Assistant Secretary for Policy Development,
United States Department of Homeland Security

Perspectives of Arif Alikhan, Assistant Secretary for Policy Development, on Community-Oriented Policing and Counterinsurgency Strategies follow.

The Department of Homeland Security (DHS) has a significant role in assisting state, local, and tribal governments in building resilience to terrorist attacks, natural disasters, violent crime, and industrial accidents. Through grant funding, assistance with planning and response, research and development, and regional coordination, DHS promotes collaborative partnerships with the numerous jurisdictions, emergency response agencies, and communities to build a stronger and safer country.

DHS believes that government and community partnerships are critical elements necessary to prevent, prepare, respond to, or recover from any catastrophic event or violent crime. This has been borne out in many circumstances where local communities, in partnership with local governments, have reduced violent crime, responded to natural disasters, and built more resilient communities to handle a variety of novel emergencies and evolving threats.

The ability of local communities, such as Los Angeles, to reduce violent crime is an excellent example of violence reduction in a complex set of circumstances involving diverse cultures, languages, needs, and governmental entities. In the past, the Los Angeles Police Department did not have the best relationship with the many diverse communities throughout the city. This was particularly acute in various low-income, culturally diverse neighborhoods in South Los Angeles where the population was predominantly African American and Latino. Major incidents from the Watts riots of 1965 to the 1992 riots following the acquittal of police officers charged with crimes in the beating of Rodney King have often been cited as manifestations of distrustful and resentful relationships between under-represented communities and law enforcement authorities.

Soon after the 1992 riots, various commissions recommended that the City of Los Angeles implement community-oriented policing approaches to building positive and constructive relationships with the communities they serve. This was not intended solely to ease racial tensions but was also seen as a mechanism to reduce the high levels of gang-related and other violent crimes that had plagued South Los Angeles for decades.

According to the U.S. Department of Justice's Office of Community Oriented Policing Services (COPS), community oriented policing involves three elements: (1) development of collaborative partnerships between police and the communities they serve; (2) collaboratively and systematically identify problems and develop prioritized and effective collaborative solutions to address the identified problems; and (3) align the organization's management, structure, and personnel to support community partnerships and proactive problem solving.

Los Angeles took many years to implement the elements of community-oriented policing and build the trust necessary for success. The investment in time, money, and structural change has resulted in dramatic reductions of violent crime, especially in gang-ridden neighborhoods. Community support for the LAPD has dramatically risen and necessary police actions, such as an officer's use of force or a series of gang-related arrests, rarely bring the public protestations and community animosity that accompanied police actions before community partnerships were developed. In addition, the positive partnerships with community members and other government agencies have resulted in an integrated whole-of-government and whole-of-community approach to the complex social phenomenon of urban crime.

There are several aspects of community-oriented policing that appear highly relevant to a successful counterinsurgency strategy. Given that counterinsurgency strategy is highly dependent on community involvement and positive relationships, the elements of community-oriented policing appear essential to success.

First, government authorities, whether military or civilian, must develop trusted and collaborative relationships with the affected populations. This requires intense study and understanding of the different cultural, ethnic, linguistic, and other backgrounds of the various communities. Often these factors not only differ significantly from city to city, village to village, but neighborhood to neighborhood and home to home. That is why it is essential that law enforcement authorities have a deep understanding of the communities they serve and a constant and consistent presence in those areas. A short deployment or rotating assignment creates significant barriers to the development of successful relationships and has often been a challenge in law enforcement agencies that frequently rotate officers or transfer officers to other assignments.

Second, constructive and collaborative partnerships between communities and authorities are necessary to develop innovative solutions to complex problems whether overseas or in the United States. Community members, who may have lived in the area for generations, will know more about their surroundings, its history, and what may or may not work to address a community problem. This has been shown time and again in U.S. communities where the communities provided innovative ideas and take an ownership role in their implementation. Similarly, a successful counterinsurgency strategy requires the indigenous population to become involved in addressing the threats they face from insurgents and others.

Third, military or police authorities involved in implementing a counterinsurgency strategy must develop a structure and systemic organizational approach to develop the expertise, provide incentives, and enable a constant and sustained presence in the community. Many police departments in the United States have proclaimed to use community-oriented policing in their communities but failed to make the organizational changes and provide the structural incentives to promote the development of the skills necessary to implement a collaborative community problem-solving approach. Successful departments, on the other hand, recruit, train, and promote officers who develop the necessary expertise. And they do so across the board, and not simply by creating a few specialty assignments within the department while the remainder of the police, who have far more interaction with the public on a daily basis, do not have the necessary skills or receive the necessary training. In fact, an untrained beat cop can often unwittingly undermine community-policing efforts and reverse any progress. A successful counterinsurgency strategy must also build into the organizations the structural and systemic elements necessary to incentivize, promote, and implement a true culture of collaborative community problem-solving.

The successes and failures of community-oriented policing in the United States can help inform the development and implementation of counterinsurgency strategies throughout the world given their similar objective of building community support to mitigate the violent actions of criminals and insurgents. This area is ripe for continued analysis, development, and refinement whether in Afghanistan or America.

Chapter 3: Visions of Conflict Policing

John Morgan

Deputy Director for Science and Technology
Counter-Terrorism Technical Support Office (CTTSO)
United States Department of Defense

Dr. John Morgan, Deputy Director for Science and Technology, the Counter-Terrorism Technical Support Office (CTTSO), the U.S. Department of Defense, chaired Roundtable I: Visions of Conflict Policing. Panel Members included Colonel Joseph Celeski and Dr. David Bayley. Colonel Celeski is Senior Fellow of the Joint Special Operations University and a former commander of coalition and joint special operations forces for two tours in Afghanistan. He is the author of the monograph: Policing and Law Enforcement in COIN—The Thick Blue Line, *a guide for newly deployed military units that provides details about the mechanics of using police to support COIN objectives to military professionals. Dr. Bayley is Distinguished Professor in the School of Criminal Justice at the State University of New York at Albany. He is the co-author with Robert Perito of the book:* Police in War, Fighting Insurgency, Terrorism and Violent Crime *that approaches the problem of a gap in curriculum and policy for training indigenous police units, especially in conflict environments.*

INTRODUCTION

It has become axiomatic that counterinsurgency (COIN) cannot be successful unless the populace is secure. Further, COIN doctrine presupposes that effective, local policing must be present to satisfy this objective. Nonetheless, very little attention has been paid to the strategies and tactics necessary to develop and use indigenous police in COIN environments. This gap exists despite the quite extensive academic literature in the two separate fields of COIN and police development. In recent years, especially (though dating back at least to T.E. Lawrence), COIN has been the subject of a great deal of discussion, leading up to the development of the seminal U.S. Army/Marine Corps *Counterinsurgency* Field Manual and its adoption as the central strategic approach of allied operations under General Petraus in both Iraq and Afghanistan.

Similarly, policing has developed a rich and influential literature over several generations of practitioner and academic contributors. From community policing and hot spots to management approaches and doctrines of legitimacy, policing theory has been debated, tested, and adopted widely into practice. Since the mid-90s, much work has been contributed to the subset of this literature that deals with the development of policing in stability operations and the developing world. For example, Bruce Baker and others have written extensively on the development of security systems, both private and public, in Africa. Nonetheless, the intersection between COIN and policing has not been widely explored, nor have the issues concerning military-police cooperation been resolved.

Two recent works attempt to address these gaps, though from very different perspectives. Colonel Joseph Celeski, Senior Fellow of the Joint Special Operations University and a former commander of coalition and joint special operations forces for two tours in Afghanistan, produced the monograph *Policing and Law Enforcement in COIN—The Thick Blue Line* as a guide for newly deployed military units. Because of the dearth of military literature on COIN, Celeski saw the need to provide details about the mechanics to military professionals of using police to support COIN objectives. Scholars David Bayley and Robert Perito also produced a book on the subject: *Police in War, Fighting Insurgency, Terrorism and Violent Crime.* Bayley and Perito approached the problem of a gap in curriculum and policy for training indigenous police units, especially in conflict environments. Materials have been developed among contractors who perform such training on behalf of the United States or United Nations, but these materials are not readily available and, in any case, do not necessarily reflect evidence-based or best practices from policing and research.

A DISCUSSION WITH CELESKI, BAYLEY, AND OTHER EXPERTS

In the interest of further developing the disparate ideas represented in these two important milestones in the development of a literature about the development of policing in COIN and other conflict environments, the National Defense University and Technical Support Working Group hosted a discussion with Celeski, Bayley, Perito and other experts concerning their research and conclusions. Because of their different perspectives, their respective conclusions contained several differences. This paper attempts to summarize their views and, to the extent feasible, provide a synthesis of their conclusions for the interested reader.

There is a long history of the development of policing in conflict environments, as well-described by Celeski and Bayley/Perito. In fact, this base of evidence is common to both viewpoints, although the examples each finds particularly instructive diverge. Celeski, for example, cites T.E.

Lawrence ("the granddaddy of COIN," as he puts it), who first postulated the insurgent paradigm: insurgents race to build their manpower while government is racing to secure the populace. The upper hand in the conflict goes to the side which is more effective in its particular race. Thus, it is self-evident that police must play a critical role in counterinsurgency as the primary mode for a government to secure its populace on a day-to-day basis. Celeski also cites success in India with the use of police forces to end an insurgency in the Punjab. Celeski notes that India has accelerated the use of police forces to deal with its Maoist Naxalite insurgency. In Andhra Pradesh, the Indian government expanded police forces by 37,000, increased intelligence gathering, and occupied what had been a power vacuum that the Naxalites had occupied for many years. This is an interesting contrast with Nepal, which was faced with the same insurgency but failed to build its police forces. Some external aid was provided to Nepal to do this, but it was insufficient or ineffective and the government fell to the Maoist insurgency over two years ago.

Celeski notes that insurgency is political warfare, where violence is used to achieve political ends. Celeski holds that COIN and violent crime are closely related, though he emphasizes their commonality as subsets of political violence in many cases. For example, most insurgencies start with criminality, i.e., as a law enforcement problem. If the police have the capacity to respond, then the situation remains stable. Also, the situation can be stabilized by reinforcement of the police, as was the case in Northern Ireland after 1976. Once the police are overwhelmed, the military will typically become involved and the violence is officially recognized as an insurgency, although the designation could easily have been applied at an earlier stage. Even at this stage, the police are usually the most impacted force. In Afghanistan, for example, according to the Special Inspector General for Afghan Reconstruction, more than twice as many members of the Afghan National Police have been killed in the war as have members of the Afghan military. Thus, Celeski insists that police be hardened with adequate physical security and supplies of weapons, as well as by military protection. Police welfare is critical, because they represent the exit strategy for COIN. Once the police can protect the public from political violence, the insurgency is fundamentally defeated. Ideally, if things are going well, one can expect that 95% of insurgents or terrorists will be brought in by policing action. Interestingly, Bayley and Perito hold a similar view. First, they agree with Celeski that the responses to insurgency, terrorism, and violent crime are closely related. They emphasize the need for police to be fair, available and responsive to respond to each of these threats. Further, they agree with Celeski that police are the "exit strategy" for COIN. However, they believe that the emphasis must be on the development of core policing that is not engaged in kinetic warfare in COIN. Rather, they believe that such "militarization" of police undermines their ties to the populace, their legitimacy, and ultimately the legitimacy of the government itself. They seek a much more brightly delineated division of labor between the indigenous military and police, as will be described in more detail below.

As a veteran of Afghanistan, Celeski has seen up close how these lessons were missed in the early years of that conflict. There was not a functioning government or police in many areas of Afghanistan for several years, and the Karzai government held little sway outside Kabul. The military, in particular the coalition military, served by necessity as a constabulary force in collaboration with tribal elders. In Afghanistan and Iraq, military operations quickly decapitated the Taliban and Baathist governments, respectively, creating a power vacuum. It was not until 2006, the so-called "Year of the Police," that a concerted effort was made in Iraq to build police forces. This was years after widespread looting and rioting in Baghdad and elsewhere that was largely unimpeded by the American military, which lacked the training, doctrine, and weapons (e.g., less lethal munitions) to deal with policing problems.

As Celeski notes, the military has many constitutional and legal reasons, such as restrictions under Title X, to refuse to do police operations, especially those related to constabulary or community policing. It should be noted that military history does not reflect bright lines between the military and police operations. Military units trained police in Indian tribal areas in the American west in the 19th Century. The Marine Corps trained police in Haiti as early as 1915. Title X itself provides that the Army peacetime mission includes counter-drug support, security assistance, and foreign internal defense, activities that are closely related to police work. In Iraq and Afghanistan, the military has been tasked to perform police training, although these activities are based on specific legal exceptions. Celeski seems to take a sanguine view of the military's police-like roles. The military performs police functions because there is no alternative. They must learn to use police tactics, train police, and use police to support COIN because that is the reality the situation demands on the ground.

Celeski advocates that military units learn the capabilities that indigenous police can provide, especially with respect to special police units. He does not suggest that police perform military operations per se, as has been done with elements of the Afghan National Police, such as the Afghan National Civil Order Police. Rather, he notes that certain police capabilities are indispensable to effective military COIN. Of course, police intelligence is a crucial tool in this regard, and the leveraging of police intelligence in

COIN is accepted universally as a critical COIN asset. Celeski goes further with the concept of "COIN-enabling" the indigenous police. First, police can substitute for the military in some sectors to free the military to be used elsewhere. Celeski favors police pseudo-operations, in which insurgents are "turned" to support the government and then sent back to the enemy camp to gather intelligence. The military, he feels, does this poorly, but a good police unit understands how to conduct snitch operations to gather intelligence. Counter-drug police have been highly effective in Afghanistan, and the American Drug Enforcement Administration has enormous experience in supporting COIN-like operations through the development of specialized, counter-drug law enforcement units, most notably in Colombia. Border patrols, paramilitary and special branch police are also useful in COIN, according to Celeski, and were critical to success in the police-led Punjabi counterinsurgency. Of course, local, community-based police units are a necessity, as outlined above, to provide the ultimate exit strategy from COIN. Their support does not necessarily conflict with the activities of special police units. Some of the activities that Celeski associates with special police units have a paramilitary flavor and the use of police in these operations may blur the lines between military and police, thus undermining police legitimacy and, by extension, the indigenous government one is seeking to support. Therefore, although these units may have some immediate utility, especially in counter-drug operations, some caution should be exercised prior to their employment or external reinforcement. It is also paramount that the training of these units emphasizes rule of law and human rights.

Celeski notes that his focus is on police and COIN, which is very different from how to manage police in stability operations or reconstruction. His thesis about the use of specialized police is very relevant to discussions of conflicts ranging from Rhodesia to Afghanistan, but one should be careful to generalize from any one of these past experiences. It is possible to see that specialized police are useful to COIN because it is necessary to use multiple strategies and tactics to defeat insurgencies. Also, by necessity, tribal police rules and expectations must be respected, and it is inadvisable to impose community or democratic ideals of policing in a tribal village. Celeski foresees that these issues will become more central to the future security environment for the United States. The core needs will be in law enforcement, intelligence, military support, and special operations. Doing these things well will be the foundation for American security after Iraq and Afghanistan wind down.

Bayley and Perito share with Celeski the importance of prioritizing indigenous police capacity-building in COIN. For them, the central questions relate to the role of the police and how they should be trained. Observing the same history and evidence as Celeski, they come to very different conclusions about the optimal strategy for the role of police in COIN. As outlined above, they share with Celeski a view that insurgency, terrorism, and violent crime form a strategic continuum with common challenges. They emphasize the need to build core policing capacity in response to each of these threats. They oppose the use of police units in military or paramilitary operations. Their three strategic principles for countering insurgency, terrorism, and violent crime are:

1. The great effectiveness multiplier in the use of state power against violence is the allegiance and support of the public.

2. In order for governments to gain public support, responsibility for security should be entrusted, in so far as possible, to police deployed among the population, who minimize the use of force and who act in accordance with accepted standards of human rights.

3. Capturing, killing, or imprisoning people committing violent acts are unlikely to be effective as a long-term solution to insecurity unless guided by precise intelligence identifying perpetrators or infrastructure.

Their first objective, focusing on the critical role of public support in COIN, is a theme shared by every modern thinker on COIN doctrine, including Celeski. The third objective, especially with respect to its emphasis on intelligence, is also a common theme. Most practitioners would agree that intelligence is critical, but would not state this necessity in the same terms as Bayley and Perito. Of course, poorly informed and planned kinetic operations can backfire and antagonize the population, as some observers believe has happened in Afghanistan. In fact, Bayley and Perito believe that kinetic operations are necessary, but that a division of labor between kinetic military operations and non-kinetic police activities is needed. One may shift from one mode to another, mixing and matching depending on security conditions, but always maintaining the role of police in serving and protecting the local population.

Thus, Bayley and Perito focus on the second objective, which implies that the development of "core" policing is the most crucial part of the COIN-policing paradigm. As Bayley has put it, the government's legitimacy can be measured by the likelihood that a parent would instruct their children to call 911 (or the equivalent) to get assistance from the police in the event of an emergency. So, the exit strategy or measure of success in COIN is the development of core policing capacity to provide essential security for the populace. Ideally, it is not necessary to implement core policing on the model of the developed, Western ideal, which is, after all, not attained universally even in the United States. Rather, for Bayley and Perito, in the context of active conflict, core policing requires that police be available, responsive, and act fairly. They view these as universal concepts that are understood in every human society. In fact, we may expect the populace to demand police who act in this way. Typically, police in COIN environments fail to be available, responsive and fair and are often corrupt, nepotic, and brutal. Such police, it may be said, will also not demonstrate loyalty to the government. We may speculate that the situation in Afghanistan would be radically different if police there were perceived to represent core policing values as outlined by Bayley and Perito.

Of course, much police training does not address the principles of core policing. Firearms training, self-protection, and law enforcement techniques dominate indigenous police training programs, whether they are sponsored by the military, civilian agencies, or the United Nations. In fact, Bayley and Perito conducted a survey of international police training programs, including some proprietary training programs given by contractors. They found that less than 10% of police training dealt with core policing values, while 50% is weapons training. Training is the opportunity to produce an attitude of service among police. Current training models fail to take the opportunity to instill those values.

What is the role of the police if they are properly trained? The government cannot deploy core police everywhere, because they will be killed. The Afghan Federal Police have two to four times the casualty rate of the Afghan National Army, and Celeski presents a range of data showing that this ratio is typical in COIN. Therefore, it is inadvisable to train police to be "little soldiers," as Bayley calls it, because police cannot be effective in kinetic COIN operations. It is difficult to fight kinetically and then shift to be responsive local police. Further, Bayley and Perito do not believe that the military should attempt police training and development. The military cannot deal with the difficult problems in building police capacity. For example, they don't have an instrument to deal with internal corruption in local forces and therefore must often just have to live with it.

If we maintain bright lines between military and indigenous police, then we must also maintain a clear division of labor as well. The military is responsible for "clearing" an area of insurgents. Both the military and police operate in the "holding" of an area. Police, on their own, are responsible for "building" security and governance. Celeski sees this division of labor in history as a natural outgrowth of weak governance, in which an insurgency grows when police are no longer capable of providing security on their own. Regardless, the local military commander must be able to make informed judgments about the division of labor in each area and the evolution of security to local police. *Thus, the success of a COIN campaign is measured by the movement of security responsibilities toward the police.* It is important to note that success cannot be measured based on the numbers of police trained or deployed. Rather, the critical performance measures are populace served by police, the populace whose security is solely provided by the police, the extent to which the military is no longer needed in holding operations, and perceptions of police accountability among the populace served.

Bayley and Perito draw some important lessons about the details of building core policing in conflict environments. As a start, local communities and ethnic groups must be engaged in the job of policing. In Los Angeles, the police recruited people who were ambassadors to their communities. Today, Latinos make up about a third of police recruits into the city police department and the perception of the police among ethnic communities has improved enormously. In Northern Ireland in 1976, the British government's Patten Commission noted that Catholic areas were under-policed, even "de-policed." Only 6% of the Royal Ulster Constabulary was Catholic, while 94% was Protestant. Not only did the direction of operations shift at that time from the military to the police, but efforts to reverse the ethnic divisions within the police were also pursued. These efforts did not make much progress until Sinn Fein was brought into the government and became a stakeholder in providing even-handed security regardless of community. This story is not yet over, and police units in some areas of Northern Ireland remain under siege. In Afghanistan, Bayley has argued that local engagement is so critical that it may be necessary to use people who "look a lot like the Taliban" but will stabilize the situation in local areas. The implication is that tribal groups can be trained and would be able to perform as available, responsive and fair police. The COIN practitioner has two choices to address tribal resistance and limitations. On the one hand, the government can devolve policing to local groups, regardless of divisions that may escalate—for a time—the visibility of divisions. Alternatively, the government can build police and other institutions that can perform across divisions using people who are trained to be fair and even-handed. We can observe that the latter approach is the primary strategy in Afghanistan, but its viability is questionable in a country with a history of almost complete local (i.e., tribal) control. Even in the days of a unified and "peaceful" Afghanistan, the central police played the role of arbiter and peacekeeper among tribal-based authorities and police units. A similar, hybrid strategy may be needed now.

Bayley and Perito highlight the issue of corruption as well. Military oversight of police capacity-building has a major weakness in this area because the military has no instrument to deal with internal corruption. As a result, American military leaders often advocate that local corruption is something "we just have to live with." Bayley and Perito point out that you can't have police that are both good and corrupt because equal protection under the rule of law is a central tenet of good policing. Therefore, the military needs alternative resources from the U.S. Government to handle civilian issues, particularly with respect to building police free from corruption. For example, one significant success of the Department of Justice ICITAP program was the development of processes to root out corruption in the Iraqi security forces.

At first glance, the Bayley and Perito and the Celeski models may appear irreconcilable. The former emphasize local, core policing and the latter the development of specialized police units that can support kinetic operations in COIN. The fundamental differences should not be ignored. Celeski sees opportunities to use police to prosecute successful COIN operations. Bayley and Perito feel that core policing has been ignored in favor of building police to support kinetic operations, thus undermining American COIN efforts. Nonetheless, there are commonalities among their views, as follows:

- COIN success can be measured by the degree to which security responsibilities have been transferred to the police. This should not be confused with metrics about the number of police or police units. Rather, this should be measured in terms of populace served and legitimacy.

- The successful COIN military commander must be aware of available police assets and maintain a strategy for the building of police capacity in his area of operations. In current operations, these assets are a critical intelligence tool to refine the targeting of insurgents. Police assets represent the central element of securing the populace, which in turn is the most important aim of COIN operations.

- Police assets should only be deployed when they can operate safely and be equipped to protect themselves. It should be expected that police will be a primary target of insurgents and will take more casualties than other units. Their physical security must be ensured if they are to be effective (and if one expects they will remain on duty).

- As a corollary to the above, military units will be needed to maintain security in an area so long as police are unable to do this job on their own. Successful COIN may be predicated on the judgment of local commanders about the proper mix of military and police assets at a particular moment in time. Further, the local commanders must judge when it is possible to pass security responsibilities to the police in a particular area.

- Civilian ("interagency") engagement is necessary to build indigenous police capacity. The military lacks the tools and doctrine to train, equip, and monitor police, so it is necessary to deploy civilian assets to perform this mission, especially in areas with communal violence.

- The training of military commanders should include collaboration with police and in the judgments needed to assist commanders in their relationship with police and in the judgments needed to share and pass security responsibilities to police in COIN or other conflict environments.

Although there are strategic differences between the two approaches, these commonalities show that there are critical lessons that may be learned from past successes and failures. In addition, from our analysis of their presentations, we may infer some ideas that are contrary to aspects in the works of either Celeski or Bayley and Perito but that may be useful syntheses.

First, the development of core policing and specialized police units may not be mutually exclusive. Specialized police units have been very successful in many conflicts, including in Afghanistan. For example, the Drug Enforcement Administration has developed specialized anti-drug police units that have interrupted the opium trade and intercepted financial flows to insurgent groups. Although these units may not be "available" or "responsive" in the traditional policing sense, they are expected to act fairly and be responsive to the Afghan populace at large. We may conclude that specialized police unit development should be a priority for COIN, so long as their training reflects the Bayley/Perito core policing doctrines as well. To be clear, Bayley and Perito do not share this view, because they feel the building of such special units interferes with the development of core policing capacity and undermines legitimacy.

Also, policy-makers should be realistic about the development of police in conflict environments. Police development must precede reconciliation among communal factions or with insurgent groups. As a result, it may be necessary to leverage local or tribal assets that have ambiguous loyalties or history to establish security in some areas. For Bayley/Perito, this could mean the development of police under local ethnic control that may, for example, have Taliban leanings but that will conform to basic concepts in the rule of law. For Celeski, this could mean the use of informants and police tactical teams to weaken insurgents. In each case, these are not just difficult choices. The situation also demands choices that may seem contrary to the ultimate objectives of national engagement but are necessary to building police capacity to protect local populations. Such choices must be made consciously and with appropriate training of those involved to minimize the possibility of abuses.

Finally, it is imperative that the United States resolve the fundamental gaps in its ability to perform the task of police capacity-building in conflict environments. From Latin America to sub-Saharan Africa to Asia, future conflicts will tend to focus on the extension of the rule of law, so the development of police will be a central need in almost every case. At present, we rely on contractor-driven training models and outdated policies that hobble both military and civilian agencies engaged with the problem. It should be noted that an ongoing, well-designed capacity in this area may have prevented much of the loss of blood and treasure in Iraq and Afghanistan of the past decade.

Although much work remains to be done on questions relating to the development of policing in conflict environments, Celeski and Bayley and Perito have made major contributions to the field. Police training and capacity-building are now the province of open academic debate. We may hope that advancement of these ideas will serve to extend peace and security in the world in coming decades.

REFERENCES

Celeski, Joseph, 2009. *Policing and Law Enforcement in COIN—The Thick Blue Line*. Hurlburt Field, Florida: Joint Special Operations University.

Bayley, H. David and Robert M. Perito, 2010. *Police in War, Fighting Insurgency, Terrorism and Violent Crime*. Boulder, Colorado: Lynne Rienner Publishers.

Chapter 4: Strategic Lessons from American Policing

Brian Berrey

Senior Advisor, Irregular Warfare Support Program (IWSP)
Combating Terrorism Technical Support Office (CTTSO)
e-mail: brian.berrey.ctr@cttso.gov

Brian Berrey is a senior advisor for the Combating Terrorism Technical Support Office's (CTTSO) Irregular Warfare Support Program (IWSP), which focuses on the research and development of non-material and material concepts and solutions for the conduct of Irregular Warfare. Panel V included three Participants: The Honorable Dr. Richard Falkenrath, former Deputy Commissioner for Counterterrorism, New York City Police Department, and Deputy Homeland Security Advisor and Deputy Assistant to the President; and with Former Charlotte Police Chief Darrel W. Stephens, who has assisted CTTSO/IWSP while serving as the President, Vice President, and Legislative Committee Chair of the Major Cities Police Chiefs Association Chief. This panel additionally hosted Mr. Jonathan Lewin, Chief Information Technologist, from the Chicago Police Department.

ABSTRACT

Regardless of the type of doctrinal term that Iraq and Afghanistan are currently framed as (COIN versus Phase IV Stability Operations), eight years into these engagements (and other Phase Zero activities), the capability gaps for population security and associated policing in conflict remains an unfulfilled requirement for the United States Government within Department of Defense as well as within the Interagency "whole of government" arena. The American Police model may not be the most adaptive, socio-political and culturally correct reproducible construct for policing in conflict; however, it has many very positive attributes, and is a reflection of what we perceive as a socially just model. A confound in COIN policing is a principal tenet of warfare in that the "enemy sets the engagement"; thus, based on the asymmetric attributes that the threat uses to destabilize fragile environments, are we, as a Nation, prepared for this new future of expeditionary Police support operations?

WHY IRREGULAR WARFARE AND POLICING IN COIN?

One of the greatest challenges DOD has is the cultural language it brings to the problems associated with Low Intensity Conflict and these "lesser wars or engagements." As these lesser engagements are more interagency or "whole of government" centric in execution, DOD can be perceived as the gorilla in the room by the country team for any support to these activities.

Regardless, DOD has devised a deep doctrinal framework to align the various sub-cultures of DOD (U.S. Army, U.S. Navy, U.S. Marine Corps, U.S. Air Force, and U.S. Special Operations). With intertwined directives and instructions, DOD can illuminate where they have a role, mission, and/or function with regard to support of anything the National Security apparatus needs to have executed; either supporting or supported.

The Irregular Warfare Joint Operational Concept (IW–JOC), as published in September 2007, pointed out that IW was a replacement for Low Intensity Conflict. Version Two[1] of the JOC did not repeat the same statement; however, framed the doctrinal discussion concerning the "five activities or operations that are undertaken in sequence, in parallel, or in blended form in a coherent campaign to address irregular threats: counterterrorism (CT), unconventional warfare (UW), foreign internal defense (FID), counterinsurgency (COIN), and stability operations (SO)."[2] Coupled to the U.S. Department of Defense Capstone Concept for Joint Operations (CCJO) what was could draw from the doctrine is a recurring critical theme of the role and importance of all blended actions that illustrate DOD's role and need to support enabling actions surrounding "protect and control civil populations and territory, improve capabilities of partners, and seek and maintain essential civil services."[3]

The presumption would could draw here is that the function of "policing" has applicability in all five activity areas of IW, not just COIN. However, in our two country engagement, that is the lens and narrative, we (the USG) are using to frame the current endeavors and discussions, i.e. we are in a COIN fight. Thus much as the famous French Officer David Galula inferenced in his writings from his Algerian experiences, counterinsurgency (COIN) is a mission for the Police, with military in support as required as is exemplified in iterative lessons learned.[4]

WHAT DID THE PANEL SAY?

DARRELL STEPHENS

Should policing be approached as a COIN strategy, and what is supposed to be the exact role of the military? Not a strategic talk; purely policing perspective. "I know policing; I don't know the military issues." It seems to me that one of the challenges we have—assuming you are going to use policing in COIN strategy—is that the military has not accepted its role as a policing entity. Does the COIN doctrine make sense and is it what we are supposed to be doing?

I thought about the urban policing strategies that may be helpful, I think policing out should be an important part of that overall perspective in stability operations, where objectives are beyond what the military objectives originally are, in helping the new governments that come into existence. There are strategies that have values, even in cultures very different from our own, since most people want to live in an environment free of violence. Policing helps bring back such sought-after stability.

"There is a lot of talk about community policing—it's the type of policing that Bayley and Perito talked about in their book—someone to respond to individual issues, someone who will treat people with fairness. The kind of policing is something that I believe will advance gains in the countries that we seek to stabilize."

A lot of work has been done in America in urban and rural environments that utilizes problem-solving principles and helps work through issues and provide safe communities. Even as far as fighting corruption—the countries we talk about have enormous levels of corruption, and local police in America have enormous levels of knowledge about this and are willing to share their experience.

Policing deals with more than just crime. Most police efforts are spent on things other than crime even though the only metric you're judged by is the crime rate. "My perception is that policing around the world is like that—they take time to resolve conflict, or intervene in conflicts, that's the kind of thing that policing brings to provide a sense of safety and security, to the extent that we possibly can." That is part of the role of the military as well. The military is expected to use force in the most economical way to achieve its objectives—protecting people or taking people into custody. Legitimacy is incredibly important in regard to policing in America, and no doubt in the rest of the world.

Stages that may be helpful to the U.S. as it approaches its operations:

- Military is not comfortable with the role it has been given in Iraq from the policing perspective.

- Military doesn't plan for the post–major operations period. It isn't normally prepared for policing or long-term stabilization efforts. We may not want this responsibility, but we got it anyway. A lot of work is done by people in the field trying to figure out the policing and security programs. Planning is a critical part.

- Military will have to play a security role initially; then you can bring in civilian experts on police training. The planning for that type of operation has to be made. "I am not arguing you have to make police officers out of soldiers—that's an unrealistic expectation." We should plan until we have civilian police capacity, at the transition point.

We have been in Afghanistan for 8 years—we could have been much further along had we given the planning more attention. Planning, building in the capacity for civilian policing, then moving toward the transition point is the natural progression of our involvement. "If we are going to make policing part of COIN ops, we have to give a lot more attention to planning than we have done in the past."

RICHARD FALKENRATH

- The military will continue to do policing—there is no alternative, it's just the reality. It's important in terms of the message such action sends to the insurgents. The DOD has to embrace the fact that the military will have to take up security/policing duties. If the actions are clearly defined, that can undermine the insurgents because they'll be identified as criminals from the beginning.

- Police training—we spend a lot of money on it in Iraq and Afghanistan, and these programs have problems. Police training is necessary but not sufficient.

- Leadership aspect is extremely important. "That is what struck me the most about NYPD," said Falkenrath. "The department I know is dependent on top-down control, in order to make sure that people do their job." Regular, everyday police duties aren't always what policemen want to do. Leadership must motivate police to do everyday work.

- Corruption is a huge problem. In the power granted to police in our society is inherent an enormous potential for abuse—we don't pay these people enough money but give them power of life and death." Natural temptation is there. It's worse if a society has a larger problem with corruption. Must design aggressive mechanisms for integrity control—policing the police, or "internal affairs." It's very hard to do, but is completely essential.

- We must design a system of checks and balances. Especially if power is centralized like it is in the NYPD, which is a large force.

- An important design question is the trade-off between centralization and efficiency or decentralization (less temptation for abuse and control) and inefficiency. You cannot have centralization of power with police that you want with your military.

- In other parts of the world, police are considered "instruments of control" for the ruling party. Police departments must be seen as apolitical; as supporting the rule of law. This is a generations-long transition, something that cannot be solved overnight.

- Force: police cannot lose. "You must maintain 'escalatory dominance'—people must know you will prevail," stressed Falkenrath. Police must have a reserve to use in dire circumstances.

- It's good for the police to come from within the community, but there is a different model. British (Indian) model, where senior officials in police are in national service. "I am not sure what is best," argued Falkenrath, "you sometimes have to parachute people in for leadership."

- Police are vital for intelligence. Know the community. Formerly arrested people are evaluated for their CI potential.

- Crime is measurable. Metrics can be tailored to regions or other filters. That is a spectacular management instrument; it's a great guidepost that informs where to deploy your resources.

CDR. JONATHAN LEWIN

- Much of policing nowadays is driven by technology and data modeling—could be used in counterinsurgency, COIN.

- CLEAR is Chicago's data modeling system, expanded to Illinois with possibility for the Greater Lakes regional system.

- Provides intelligence to everyday patrol officers. Data relayed from real-time crime center. Web 2.0 map is used for event intelligence tracking. Everyone in the department has access to this information.

- Interactive maps are quickly navigated/created.

- FIMS used by all first responders in the city. Call center is linked to the analysts in the Crime Prevention Information Center who then filter the information—technology fusion center.

- Technology fusion center—connecting the dots between all the data.

- Reportable uses of force: complaints, minor infractions, awards, citizen contacts, injury on duty, ratio of complaints to arrests, all tracked live. This is updated every day.

- The system can rank-order various buildings through agglomerations of data between agencies in order to monitor troubled areas.

- Blackberry PDAs pilot program: "Officers love it." 800 Blackberrys are currently in circulation.

- Would like to expand problem-solving techniques with the community. Researching possibilities of real-time camera-sharing between citizens and police. 3,500 camera-related arrests so far, where camera-share played a role.

- Automated system can track if the camera played a role in the arrest. And anyone can send us a crime tip by text messages, just by using a phone.

- Current state—data action state, where we can generate maps. Would like to build systems for crime prediction by compiling data in model. We want to be proactive by utilizing any data source that we can get that we can legally use. We are trying to generate maps predicting where things may occur.

PANEL QUESTIONS AND ANSWERS

Q: So many police officers are almost like overlapping tribes with their own jurisdictions. There are formal and informal arrangements that govern them. We don't try to replicate that in places like Afghanistan where tribal authority already exists. How does NYPD operate in that regard?

A: In the U.S. we have a unifying principle, which is the rule of law. They operate along same Constitutional guidelines. Another answer: "I would not design the system like we have." I would also not design a national police system for our country either. Some combination of local to state to federal makes a lot of sense here and in other countries as well. Some tribal jurisdiction may work if we can "keep them honest" to adhere to the rule of law.

Q: All three of you manage large municipal police organizations. Is there a way that large police organizations can participate in burden-sharing, how realistic is it, and can we make it work?

A: It's a great idea, but in practice it does not work because we have no slack. Policing in the U.S. is a 24-7-365 job; we have no reservoir for additional resources; it will have to be a major federal effort of some kind—people are busy, working every day. We have a small effort in Haiti, but the department is too busy.

Q: Would there be a potential, if a funding source was available, to build out an international-type capability. Is the limitation money or a bureaucracy?

A: There are risks—officers can get hurt in foreign countries. We are
     not configured to support expeditionary expeditions. But we are
     now down 60,000 cops since 9-11 (in NYC). When you hire a cop
     in NYC, it's a multimillion-dollar proposition, which entails
     enormous resources. Yes, there is a price, but its a high price at
     which a federal government can potentially make a deal with the
     police department. It is the right concept, since this is where the
     expertise is. It is a theory, but it does not work in practice. For
     example, in Haiti, police left the U.S. and came back safely, but
     police were there for a little while. It's an enormous burden on
     police forces to make up for the short fall for the police that can be
     deployed overseas. This nation can be at a unique time to take a
     look at some international models, like the Australian or a European
     model. But how does it help local police departments if some cops
     may want to go overseas and we have to make up for the shortfall?
     How about hiring a civil servant in that role with pension and
     benefits?

DO WE KNOW WHAT WE HAVE DONE SO FAR?

As this symposium was focused on Operation Enduring Freedom–
Afghanistan (OEF–A), and leveraging Operation Iraqi Freedom (OIF)
experiences, one shortfall identified was the capture of the number of
activities undertaken across the services, and interagency partners, in pursuit
of developing a body of knowledge with regard to Policing in a COIN
Environment. Anecdotal discussions, as well as contracted support activities,
have been executed since 2005. A sampling includes the following:

*   Mobile Embedded Tactical Reconnaissance Operations
    (METRO); a look at Police Methodologies for combating
    Revolutionaries and Gangs. (DIA/CTTSO effort in Iraq, 2004).

*   Army Science Board, Police Capacity Development—Do We
    Understand the Dilemma, 2005. (RRTO/DIA/CTTSO effort
    with ASB).

*   COIN—Technical Surveillance Architecture support effort
    deploying technical tactical information collection means to 1/7
    MEB as it deployed into Al Qaim in 2005 with embedded
    LAPD advisor/trainer support. (RRTO/JIEDDO/CTTSO
    effort).[5]

- General Petraeus FM 3–24 rewrite and establishment of the COIN Center at Fort Leavenworth (2005–2007).

- Pinellas County Sheriff's Office Symposiums of Law Enforcement Support to DOD Operations, conducted through CTTSO/TSWG and IWSP. (*See attached reports*).

- Legacy—Police Informant and Information Business Processes training for Iraqi Ministry of Interior, in support of U.S. Marine Corps in Al Anbar, 3rd ID in MND (2006–2010). (JIEDDO/RRTO/IWSP effort).

- Law Enforcement Program—Embedded Law Enforcement Advisors to Brigade Combat Commanders. (JIEDDO effort).

SO WHAT HAVE WE LEARNED?

Opinions vary, perspectives are provided from where one sits; from inside the USG—Allied Nation engagement arena in OEF–A and OIF, to host partner nation capabilities and capacities to absorb the "dogma du jour." Inconsistency in approach exists based on the local dynamics and threat conditions, as well the receptivity of rule of law development to support population security and economic development in "parting the insurgents from the rest of the fish in pond." At times one could perceive that the interagency is not synchronized in the construct of what "Policing in COIN" means.

As a research and development program office that has pursued non-material solutions in this space, it has been stated by Department of State that policing in conflict is beyond their scope of capability. Couple to this the understanding that "policing" as a complex capability does not mean the same thing to many foreigners as it is understood in the Western Hemisphere. In many countries, police are tied to the Ministry of Interior and are a tool to suppress the population, not necessarily to protect and serve.

In OIF and OEF–A, DOD has opted for a Police imbed Training Team (PiTT) construct coupled together with rapid indigenous Police indoctrination and training capabilities to assist in capacity development for an element of establishing the Rule of Law. The other components of the Rule of Law (detainee operations and courts) lagged far behind this rudimentary development of patrolmen. A common perception is that American military and irregular warfare actions should leverage methods developed in policing to interdict insurgent or terrorist activity and enhance legitimacy of friendly governments through extension of the rule of law; which some of is alluded to in the doctrinal writings within the IW–JOC. However, the IW–JOC also identifies in Stability Operations that "the Department of State and the U.S. Agency for International Development (USAID) will be the lead U.S. agencies to support a host-nation's effort to establish or improve key aspects of governance to include rule of law and a variety of services."[6]

One of the most critical aspects that is probably not understood to the integration of the role of "Rule of Law" in the past two engagements has been the timing and sequencing of when, where, and who supports development and sustainment activities of police, courts, and prisons in a fluid "seize, clear, build" COIN fight. These engagements, and development activities, are never uniform across a conflict zone.

It could be easily opined that what we, as a DOD entity, are really learning was better captured during this workshop lunchtime sharing discussions with National Defense University students providing a sharing perspective. The better question may be "are they concerned with the Policing in COIN" aspects and if not then what were they concerned with?

WHAT HAVE WE MISSED?

As illustrated in the Panel member's comments; many who have contributed from the Law Enforcement community to Department of Defense with time, personnel, and insights; the lack of documented understanding of what we have done so far becomes one of the greatest challenges in being prepared to not repeat the costs of what we should have learned from a force application, preparedness and doctrinal perspective.

This is illuminated by solid contextual frame of writings that exist with regard to understanding what is required in Low Intensity Conflict and post-conflict stages. Most notably, the Rand Corporation COIN studies present a wide body of literature on the subject. Additionally, the prospect of the international community implied moral obligation of "you broke it, now you must fix it" in these expeditionary engagements, which resulted in Presidential Decision Directive 56 in 1997 on "Managing Complex Contingency Operations" and then eight years later National Security Presidential Directive 44, "Management of Interagency Efforts Concerning Reconstruction and Stabilization." A culmination of these experiences was released by Rand in 2007 with former Ambassador Dobbins (and team) release of "The Beginners Guide to Nation-Building," which capitalized on other work with an experiential-based framework of considerations and planning factors for nation-building.

Whether it be the failing, or failed, state situation or a transition to reconstruction and stability process, the monograph is an essential primer for understanding force constructs and relationships required to assist in planning the elements associated with not only Policing aspects, but the inter-related aspects of nation-building activities inclusive of governance, economic stabilization, and more.[7]

Added to this complex issue is the fundamental gap that the U.S. Military has been disconnected from this function based on historical aspects leading back to Viet Nam–era foreign policy issues. A very good treatise on the subject illuminating the gap inside the U.S. military and the Interagency is found in the U.S. Army Peacekeeping and Stability Operations Institute (PKSOI) Paper from the Army War College in Carlisle titled "U.S. Military Forces and Police Assistance in Stability Operations: The Least-Worst Option To Fulfill the U.S. Capacity Gap," by retired Colonel Dennis E. Keller. The artful discussion makes a solid case concerning the change in environment, and engagements in a globalized market space and commons may require re-looking at the prohibitions outlined in the Foreign Assistance Act of December 1974 inclusive of Section 660.[8] USAID now supports community based policing endeavors as approved through the 2005 Foreign Operations, Export Financing, and Related Program Appropriations Act. The author points to the difference and the need for stability policing as a precursor to community based policing.[9]

WHAT ARE FUTURE DIRECTIONS?

The ongoing COIN operation in Afghanistan will continue for the foreseeable future as DOD programming has funding identified well out past 2014. Regardless of the force configuration on the ground, the need to support the continued transitional aspects of reconstruction and stability inclusive of security sector support will endure and grow.

One sitting in the discussion could distinctly feel the dichotomy emerge between practitioners from a DOD-centric community, and those who have worked the Law Enforcement community based model in lesser conflicts from outside DOD. The cultural separation inside the conference room may have reflected the dilemma that exists on the ground forward and will exist in future scenarios, especially in light of the changing globalized threat.

The recurring theme about the globalized threat and how the nexus between criminality, terrorism, gangs and illicit trafficking point to a future greater need and a more robust scrutiny and understanding of roles and missions. A recent monograph on the subject even suggests that organized crime in a failing state could be identified as a form of irregular warfare.[10] Nation-state weak institutions and the ability of non-state actors to erode the authority and the "social contract"[11] with the population will emerge as one of the most critical elements of planning for the next twenty years. The discourse within the Interagency concerning Security, Stabilization, Transition, and Reconstruction (SSTR) versus Security Sector Reform/Development (SSR/D) and what it means to the U.S. as a National Security issue is a critical imperative in addressing what this workshop sought to at least put a bit of light on. "Security is a core obligation under international law, a core service that is demanded by citizens, and the foundation for sustainable economic and social development. Support for security sector reform (SSR) should be undertaken within a framework of rule of law and through reinforcement of the state-society contract and, thus, the legitimacy of the state."[12]

The complexity of providing a U.S. engagement construct is problematic as the issue is a "political activity,"[13] and understanding what its relationship to the social contract between state and its citizens is crucial.

What we can say here at this point is that we have invested heavily in trying to understand what is needed. This is a unified, partner nation, and non-governmental organization–supported mission. DOD can provide a bridge; but the rest of the partners are required to be successful. Now the question becomes; how do we build that logical U.S. Government framework and bridging capacity for the future and what does it look like?

REFERENCES

1. *Irregular Warfare: Countering Irregular Threats, Joint Operational Concept*; Version 2.0; 17 May 2010.

2. Ibid., 5.

3. Ibid., 10.

4. *OEF-P Counterinsurgency Best Practices;* Combined Arms Center Blog; http://usacac.army mil/blog/blogs/llop/archive/2009/05/27/oef-p-counterinsurgency-best-practices.aspx (last accessed 21 Oct 10).

5. Russell, James A., 2010. *Innovation in War: Counterinsurgency Operations in Anbar and Ninewa Provinces, Iraq, 2005–2007*; *The Journal of Strategic Studies* 33, no. 4, August 2010, 597–603.

6. IW–JOC, 19.

7. Dobbins, James, Seth G. Jones, Keith Crane, Beth Cole DeGrasse, 2007. *The Beginner's Guide to Nation- Building*; Rand Monograph; http://www rand.org/pubs/ monographs/MG557 (last accessed 29 Oct 10).

8. Keller, Colonel (Ret.), Dennis E., August 24, 2010. *U.S. Military Forces and Police Assistance in Stability Operations: The Least-Worst Option to Fill the U.S. Capacity Gap*, 6–7, http://www.strategicstudiesinstitute.army mil/pubs/display.cfm?pubID= 1013 (last accessed 29 Oct 10).

9. Ibid., iii and 11.

10. *Crime, Violence, and the Crisis in Guatemala: A Case Study in the Erosion of the State*. Brands Hal, 2010, 3, http://www.strategicstudiesinstitute.army mil/pubs/ display.cfm?PubID=986 (last accessed 23 Oct 10).

11. *From Fragility to Resilience: Concepts and Dilemmas of State building in Fragile States*; A Research Paper for the OECD Fragile States Group Submitted by the Center on International Cooperation at New York University & International Peace Academy; 4 March 2008; 3–5, Argument Section para 1–15, http://www.cic.nyu. edu/global/docs/fragilitytoresilience.pdf (last accessed 27 Oct 2010).

12. Ibid., 31.

13. Scheye, Eric, 2010. *United States Institute of Peace Special Report: Realism and Pragmatism in Security Sector Development*, 2, http://www.usip.org/publications/ realism-and-pragmatism-in-security-sector-development (last accessed 24 Oct 10).

The views expressed in this report do not necessarily reflect the views of the National Defense University, Department of Defense, or Combating Terrorism Technical Support Office, which do not advocate specific policy positions.

Chapter 5: Lessons Learned from Iraq and Afghanistan Operations

Samuel Musa

Senior Research Fellow
Center for Technology and National Security Policy
National Defense University

Samuel Musa, Senior Research Fellow at the Center for Technology and National Security Policy, the National Defense University, chaired a Roundtable that discussed Lessons Learned from operations in Iraq and Afghanistan. During the Roundtable, presentations were made by five students from the National War College (NWC) and the Industrial College of the Armed Forces (ICAF). The students had extensive experience in theater operations and were ready to share their lessons learned. Commander Peter Phillips, Naval Special Warfare, a student at the National War College, a Joint Task Force Commander in 2009, commanding ten maneuver elements to include seven with OGA support, and a total of 900 joint forces on the ground, discussed the differences between COIN operations in Iraq and Afghanistan. Colonel Darrel Wilson, a student at ICAF, discussed the provincial reconstruction teams, focusing on governance and development. Colonel Wilson worked on the operational level with ISAF, doing mostly tactical tasks and had 14 months of experience in Afghanistan (2007–2008) in Regional Command South. His focus was on the development of the Afghan National Army, Afghan National Police, and Provincial Reconstruction Teams. Commander Mark Fedor, USCG, a student at NWC, had experience with counternarcotics operations in the Caribbean and had worked at the House of Representatives Drug-Policy subcommittee oversight of DoD counternarcotics efforts, discussed narcotics trafficking in Afghanistan and its impact on the effectiveness of government programs. Commander Wilson Marks, USN, a student at NWC and a PRT Commander in Afghanistan from July 2009 to March 2010, and then at ISAF Joint Command in Kabul from March 2010 to July 2010, discussed his experience in the Kandahar region. Vangala Ram, a student at ICAF from the Department of State, was in Afghanistan for 16 months in 2007–2008 and was responsible for State programs, as well as the military equipment programs, discussed problems caused by lack of cultural awareness and corruption.

INTRODUCTION

There are several books and manuals dealing with the counterinsurgency operations in Iraq and Afghanistan operations.[1-7] The literature is also full of papers on lessons learned from these operations. The purpose of this chapter is not to summarize what has already been published but rather to focus on the deliberations of a roundtable held on this subject at the workshop on Policing and Counterinsurgency Operations held at NDU on September 29, 2010. However, it is important to highlight some of the major publications on the subject with emphasis on the relationship of policing and counterinsurgency.

One of the major publications is the counterinsurgency guide issued by the government in January 2009 and signed by the Secretary of Defense, the Secretary of State, and the Administrator of USAID.[8] It is a high level document: A synthesis of counterinsurgency theory with recent experience across the U.S. Government. It also focuses on integrated operations that apply civilian and military capabilities across information, security, political and economic functional areas. The document identifies Physical security as only one step toward "Human Security," which is maintenance of laws, human rights, freedom to conduct economic activity, public safety, and health.

Another major release is by General Petraeus, who issued his counterinsurgency guidance in July 2010.[9] It has many elements, but the ones dealing with relationship-building and potentially policing are listed here:

- Secure and serve the population.
- Live with the people.
- Build relationships, but not just with those who seek you out.
- Be a good guest—help the community.
- Walk—engage the population.

In the area of securing and serving the population, General Petraeus said, "We have learned that the only way to secure the population is to live with it. You cannot commute to the fight in a place like Iraq. We have to put our forces, together with those of our coalition partners and our host-nation counterparts, in the neighborhoods whose occupants we are striving to secure. Often, this is where the violence is the greatest. But when we do that and the people realize that we are there to stay, they typically begin to provide information on the enemy; often, they also volunteer to help hold areas once we have cleared them." Furthermore, he highlighted that "we have to understand the people, their culture, their social structures and how systems to support them are supposed to work—and how they do work. And our most important tasks have to be to secure and to serve the people, as well as to respect them and to facilitate the provision of basic services, the establishment of local governance and the revival of local economies."

One of the co-authors with General Petraeus, of the U.S. Army/Marine Corps *Counterinsurgency Field Manual*, is John Nagl. He cited in *World Politics Review*[10] that "The lessons learned are: You have to protect the population first. And learn and adapt. What General Petraeus and his team did in Iraq over the past two years was those two things. They focused first on protecting the population. But they also had a flexible and agile mindset that constantly evaluated where they were and what they wanted to accomplish and tried to figure out the best way forward based on the continually evolving situation on the ground. And it was that mindset that allowed Petraeus' team to take advantage of things like the Sunni Awakening through outreach to the tribes."

More recently, Secretary of Defense Robert Gates, on November 23, 2010, approved a list of essential counterinsurgency (COIN) skills that troops need to be successful in Afghanistan.[11] The COIN Qualification Standards are a list of nine major skill areas with roughly 52 subtasks meant to focus units' training before they deploy to Afghanistan. The list contains the following skill areas:

- Receive basic individual Afghan-specific COIN education.

- Understand the operational environment.

- Conduct relief in place.

- Conduct decentralized operations.

- Partner with Afghanistan national security forces.

- Conduct information operations.

- Create conditions for stability.

- Conduct detainee operations.

- Develop a learning organization.

In order to examine the role of policing in counterinsurgency, it is important to begin with the basics. The main problem is to provide information relevant to the human terrain in COIN operations. The military/intelligence community has the resources to provide actionable intelligence based on the extensive resources available. The police can provide information based on trust/legitimacy. There are four options available:

1. Train the military in policing tactics. The Marines and SOF do it well, while the Army has a long way to go.

2. Utilize police as an adjunct to operations. JIEDDO has police personnel assigned to specific battalions.

3. Police take responsibility for the entire operation with visibility upfront and military as backup. Services may object to their secondary role.

4. Police and military assume different lanes.

The principal factors are time and money. If time is not an issue, then all the above options can be accomplished. However, the policymakers provide time constraints on when the overall mission needs to be completed and forces removed from the country. This constraint then favors the top two options listed above.

The police have played an important role in current and past counterinsurgency operations. In fact, the police can assume different roles depending on the organization. The centralized police force in Iraq did not work well due to the lack of professionalism as well as trust. They work well in developed countries. By the middle of 2009, the Iraqi National Police (INP) had become an effective counterinsurgency force.[12] However, this made it difficult as to whether it is a military or police force. The INP had little connection to the judicial system and its procedures. The local police force is generally corrupt and the justice system needs major changes to make it effective. The private local police force is efficient and works well in many countries for providing protection to citizens and businesses. Then there is the use of militia for neighborhood watch. They worked well but they do not have accountability and as result they are not acceptable to the Western World.

The challenges of policing in Afghanistan are the low literacy rate, high attrition, corruption, low pay, and lack of training. The literacy rate is about

14%, which makes it difficult to ensure that the rules of law and the basics of policing are well understood. The high attrition rate of the police force of 70% per month makes it impossible to keep any semblance of continuity and professionalism. New initiatives have taken place to reduce the attrition rate to about 40%, which is still high. The low pay is being addressed so that at least it is compatible with what the Taliban pays for its police counterparts. It is estimated that 40% of the police are not trained in the basics of policing. New initiatives are also underway to correct this situation. The Afghan Local Police Initiative (ALP) is managed by the Ministry of Interior with initial capability of 10,000. New professional police education programs are also being developed. The Afghanistan security system is further complicated by the assignment of several nations to oversee support and reforms. More specifically, the U.S. was assigned the responsibility of the military; Germany, the police; Italy, the judiciary; and Great Britain, the counternarcotics. The Afghan National Police was being pulled into the four disjoint sectors.

In both Iraq and Afghanistan, creating and sustaining a police force during an insurgency is difficult. It requires a national army and some form of a national level paramilitary police force. The paramilitary police force can impose security while the local police force can enforce it locally. This also means that local and national institutions will have to be created to support them. In addition, a judicial system with proper legislation, courts, judges, and other personnel will have to be in place to take care of local disputes and crimes that are committed. The prisons and confinement systems will have to be properly designed and operated so as not to provide an incubation facility for insurgencies and radicalization. There is a need for a rule of law, particularly in Afghanistan. The Afghan National Army (ANA) has a judicial system that is well-resourced with international advisors under a unified command, while the civilian court system lacks the leadership and resources. Low pay for prosecutors and judges has led to corruption. There is a need for a single entity to oversee all facets of the rule of law.[13] One option is to utilize the command structure provide by the International Stabilization Assistance Force (ISAF). Another option is to utilize the State Department combined interagency task force (CJIATF).

PANEL DELIBERATIONS

The Dean of Students at NWC and ICAF identified a number of students who served recently in theater. The Roundtable was fortunate to have five students from the National War College and the Industrial College of the Armed Forces. The students had extensive experience in theater operations and were ready to share their lessons learned. The speakers were asked to describe their role in theater operations including location and timeframe. They were asked to provide comments on any of the three questions:

1. Based on your own experience, what was the role of the military and the police in the operations? Do you have examples of operations that worked well and those that did not?

2. What were the main obstacles and what are the solutions?

3. In your opinion, what should be the roles of the police and military in theater and in combined operations? Should the military be trained in policing methods?

COMMANDER PETER PHILLIPS

First, Commander Peter Phillips, Naval Special Warfare, and a student at the National War College, opened the panel discussion. He was a Joint Task Force Commander in 2009, commanding ten maneuver elements to include seven with OGA support, total 900 joint forces on the ground. Additionally, he also served in OIF and HOA.

Commander Phillips stated that Afghanistan was, and still is, a lot of work. There is a big difference when it comes to COIN operations in Iraq and in Afghanistan. Once everyone arrived to Iraq, everyone had the same goal to have a stable democracy. The U.S., coalition forces and different agencies all looked at the WMD program, regional stabilization, and/or violation to U.N. It was good that everyone had the same goal, including the Iraqis. While there were many reasons to go to Iraq, there was a single goal in the end as to why everyone was there; nationalism was very important and was useful in overcoming religion and tribalism.

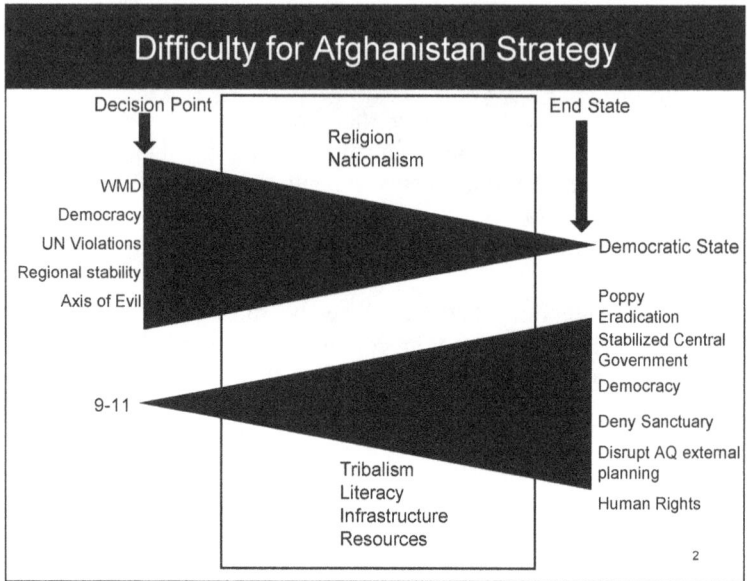

Figure 1: The Difficulty for an Afghanistan Strategy.

The Afghanistan mission was decided upon after 9/11. There were no unifying strategies in the coalition because everyone had different priorities and RoEs (Figure 1). Depending on who you talked to, there were multiple reasons for being there. Depending on the year you went, the resources and strategy changed. Commander Phillips stated that from a military ground perspective it was unclear of the overall strategic mission. Stabilization of the central government and disruption of Al Qaeda's external plans were all extremely important. Sometimes his own mission was detrimental to the other organization's mission. Tribalism and literacy problems worked against U.S. efforts as well. There is no structure in Afghanistan—there were no roads during the first year and a half. Resources there were terrible!

While the overall strategy was to support the national goals, his work was to support the General (Figure 2). "What is the strategy for Afghanistan? We had no answer." So what do we do? Pump our resolve, drain the enemy's, attract the uncommitted to our side—such as remove Al Qaeda and Taliban senior leaders from the battlefield; disrupt networks, or end conflict on favorable terms?"

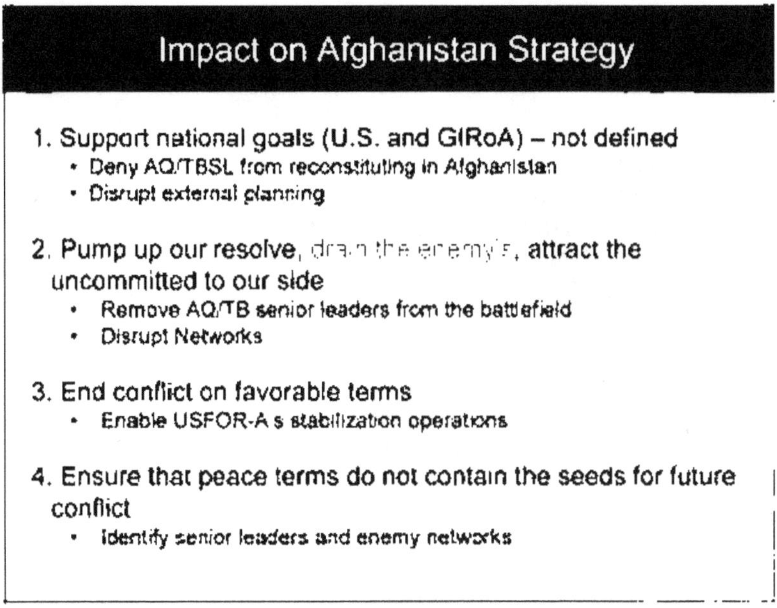

Impact on Afghanistan Strategy

1. Support national goals (U.S. and GIRoA) – not defined
   - Deny AQ/TBSL from reconstituting in Afghanistan
   - Disrupt external planning

2. Pump up our resolve, drain the enemy's, attract the uncommitted to our side
   - Remove AQ/TB senior leaders from the battlefield
   - Disrupt Networks

3. End conflict on favorable terms
   - Enable USFOR-A s stabilization operations

4. Ensure that peace terms do not contain the seeds for future conflict
   - Identify senior leaders and enemy networks

Figure 2: The Impact on Afghanistan Strategy.

The actions on the ground reflected a change in military mission over the course of the war. Despite what some might have said was the mission, those actions reflected the following strategy (Figure 3).

- From October 2001 to February 2002: the mission was to kill and capture AQ; remove Taliban as the government of GIRoA.

- February 2002 to 2005: AQ and Taliban leadership in Pakistan; Security Operations (securing lines of communication, etc.), forward operating bases, stability of the patrons.

Military Strategy

1. Oct 2001 – Feb 2002
   - Kill and Capture AQ
   - Remove Taliban as government of GIRoA
2. Feb 2002 – 2005
   - AQ and Taliban leadership in Pakistan
   - Security Operations
     - Forward Operating Bases
     - Stability patrols
3. 2005 – 2009
   - Save Afghanistan (Kill and Capture Taliban)
   - Develop an Afghanistan Army
4. 2009 – TBD
   - COIN
   - Reconciliation considered

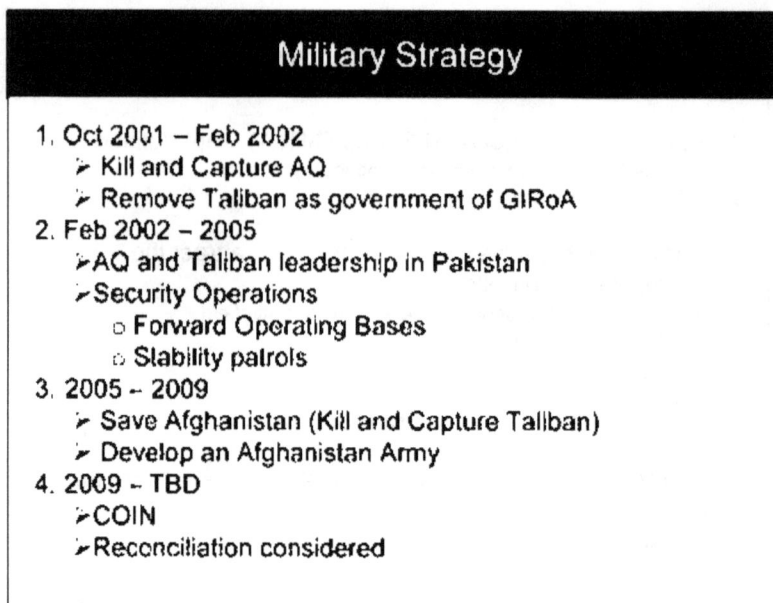

Figure 3: Military Strategy for Afghanistan.

- 2005–2009: Save Afghanistan (kill/capture Taliban); develop Afghanistan Army—depending on who a person was affects the making of Security Forces to protect your bases, VIPS, etc. There was an army before 2005, but afterwards, the strategy was "stop what you are doing" and let's gets everyone on board. Prior to 2005, depending on who you were, you were building up your own security forces. Unfortunately, the Rules of Engagement were not consistent.

- The use of militias was a necessary security factor. From 2009 onwards, COIN strategy and reconciliation considered (really had to wait till 2010 to talk of reconciliation to a General).

Building freedom of action was critical (Figure 4). A person's ability to move around is very important. If one cannot move around with the Afghan people or understand different cultures, you will not survive. Commander Phillips underscored that "if you can't move, they [the enemy] will. If they can say you are doing bad things, then you are [doing them]. You can't have COIN unless you have freedom of action."

Commander Phillips stressed the need for a unified structure as part of the overall mission. Coalition Chain of Command—when we look at a military strategy, who actually controls what? What does a senior officer actually control (Figure 5)? Everyone had a different chain of command. "It's like saying that the United States is a unified country because we have one President, and all police agencies in the country work as one—that is simply not true." Since various chains of command were working parallel to each other, there was no overall unity. The idea of a "top-down perspective" will not work in Afghanistan UNLESS you unify the chain of command. "In Ireland, everyone worked for one guy—whether you are police, intelligence, etc., everyone worked for him. We don't have that in Afghanistan."

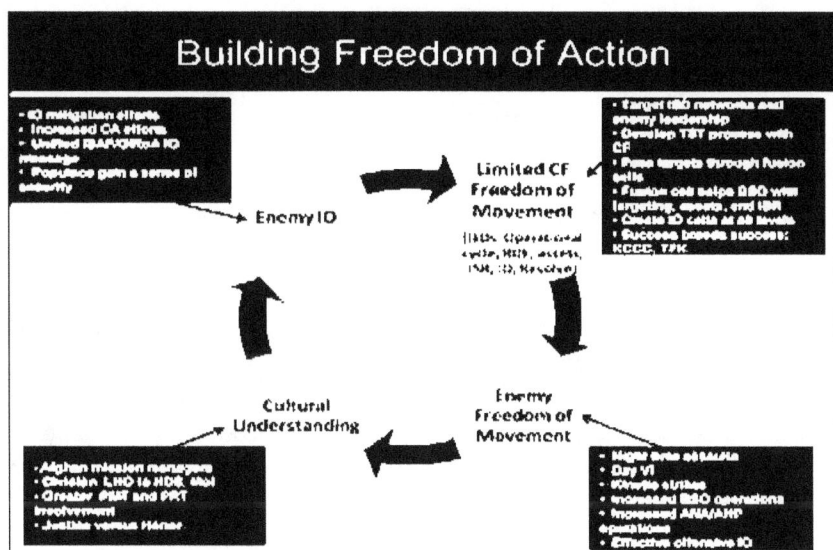

Figure 4: Building Freedom of Action.

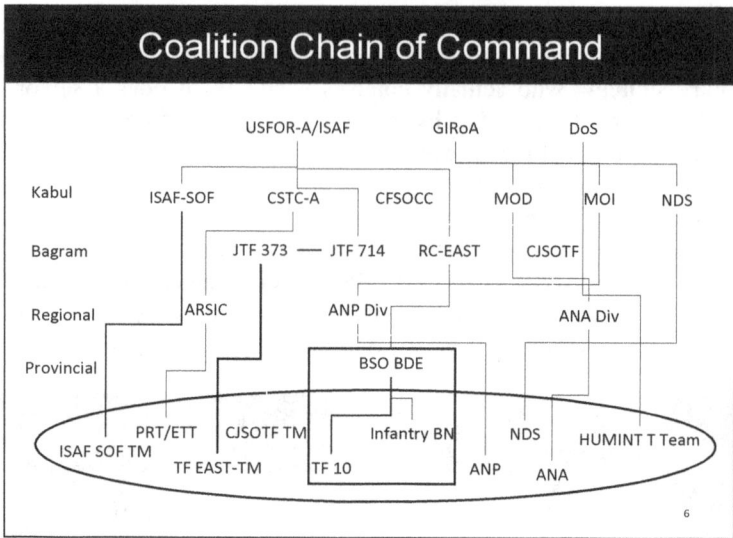

Figure 5: The Coalition Chain of Command.

COLONEL DARREL WILSON

Second, Colonel Darrel Wilson, a student at ICAF, discussed the Provincial Reconstruction Teams (PRTs)—focusing on governance and development. Colonel Wilson worked on the operational level with ISAF, doing mostly tactical tasks. His focus was on the development of the Afghan National Army, Afghan National Police, and Provincial Reconstruction Teams. He had 14 months of experience in Afghanistan (2007–2008) in Regional Command South. He served as the senior advisor to Major General Jamaludin in Zabul Province. He worked closely with the Provincial Reconstruction Team and other Agencies. He participated in all meetings between the Afghan Commander and the Governor.

Stability operations—(governance and development); the security line of operation is intertwined with everything that you do. We had Army, Navy, Air Force and National Guard soldiers, a Romanian training team and a US-led PRT, including interagency pieces, like State Department and Department of Agriculture personnel embedded with the team in Zabul Province; these staffers had more experience on the ground than he had, including many years working in various countries. "We had to work closely with agriculture and development teams, as well as with special forces. We tried to coordinate efforts as best we could. It was important to talk as colleagues instead of having an 'I am your boss' attitude," commented Wilson.

Colonel Wilson's concerns involved policing. Within our PRT, we used a civil affairs team to mentor/partner with the police in certain areas. The idea of embedding such a mentoring team was EXTREMELY important; they talked to the chiefs of police and taught a "community policing" class, including showing the locals how to interact. We would review the local's actions afterwards—it worked well. Little progress was made when the police were of a different ethnic background than the local population. The good thing was that we had the autonomy to implement this on our own. The sad part was that we did it all on our own, without the direction from above. His concern was also how to build a police force now that the Afghan Armed Forces were stood up. Community Policing—how do you talk to the people you are supposed to be protecting?

COMMANDER MARK FEDOR

Commander Mark Fedor, USCG, student at NWC, spoke next. His experience was with counternarcotics in the Caribbean. He worked at the House of Representatives Drug-Policy subcommittee oversight of the DoD counternarcotics efforts, including what is taking place in Afghanistan with the poppies. In the fall of 2006, he was part of a Congressional staff that went to Pakistan, Afghanistan, and Tajikistan to examine the heroin problem.

The question of the Afghanistan drug problem soon arose, but the House Staff was not that familiar with the drug problem in 2006 (not at the top of the list), so Commander Fedor went to Pakistan, Afghanistan, and Tajikistan to get a better look. Drug trade is big business—you have to acknowledge that it's a problem. Lots of lessons have emerged from counternarcotics activities in the Caribbean—the main one being that when the drugs are running rampant in the country, the government programs' effectiveness will be limited.

There are connections between drug traffickers, terrorists, and insurgents. They receive the money and protection they need to move their products. As we travel in the region, we know that the drugs are flowing overseas. The answer was to think of the problem like a water balloon. When a person squeezes the balloon at one end it will pop in the other end. In other words, the U.S. needed to start thinking ahead of them. Officials cannot just focus on one country or one province because when you stop in one area it will go to the next. Those drugs are flowing like crazy into

Russia, Europe, etc., the speaker explained. We needed to start looking at the whole perspective, not just law enforcement or military, but DoD and DEA. The idea was for all of these agencies to work together—which is not as easy as one would think.

At the time, officials believed that the best way to combat all the drugs was aerial spraying. From the law enforcement perspective that seems easy, but the DoD does not use its assets like that—it needs a protocol, while the DEA was ready to go and grab drug labs. But we also learned that the Afghans did not like aerial spraying because it made many of them think back to the days of the Russians. So how do we eradicate the fields? We tried to do it on the ground, but our people were easy targets. Then, officials were given ATVs to disperse spray through fields. This also did not last long because it was unsafe. The number of hectares cultivated for poppies went down, but the amount of heroin was still high—the overall problem was still going strong because of the previously stated "balloon theory"—stop activities in one area and they go to the next.

The overall process needs to produce an alternative means for the farmers to make money. Farmers just want to feed their families and they can get money from the drug business. What incentives can be produced to make the farmer move away? DoD and DEA tried to get agriculture involvement, even bring in farmers from the U.S. to speak with the locals. Lastly, there was a bridge built in order to increase commerce between Afghanistan and Tajikistan—but who will do the customs and who will monitor the commerce and flow of narcotics?

COMMANDER WILSON MARKS

Commander Wilson Marks, USN, a student at NWC, next discussed his experience in Kandahar region. He was a PRT Commander in Afghanistan from July 2009 to March 2010 and then at ISAF Joint Command in Kabul from March 2010 to July 2010. From October 2007 to December 2008, Commander Marks was responsible for Training, Mentoring, and Advising, primarily the Afghan Army. If you stayed long enough you can say it has gotten a lot better since before in all aspects, but not the police. Governance overall has made very little progress. His forces developed their own campaign strategies; basically sell the plan for local support. The plan went across everything, such as judicial, economic, education, infrastructure, development, law enforcement; all together, strategy upfront was needed. We had no unity of command; we had the unity of effort.

The biggest lesson while stationed in Afghanistan for Commander Marks was that it is the Afghans' lives, their country, and it has to be the Afghans' solutions. The Afghan citizens are not going to adopt our way of thinking. We have to help them to understand there is another way to look at it, give them some tools that they can use, be active in their interactive session, and then help them execute it and back them up when they fall down. In other words, the U.S. and coalition forces need to train and implement at the same time.

The roads turned into "tolls" and the military and police would charge people to drive through close to 60 check-points on the main road where he served. To combat this easy way to make drug money was to pull everyone off the highway and to essentially establish a "neighborhood watch" concept.

The fact that we were able to secure polling stations was another huge plus. The election commission wanted to put polling stations in areas that were just not going to be supported. When the Taliban is physically in control of an area, why would you put a polling station in that area? District centers: the government appointed district chiefs, but locals would not recognize their authority. Afghan citizens would look at family orientation and their old tribal leaders, not the province leaders put into place at district centers. "We were on a steep cliff automatically because of that." We ended up in securing those district centers, but at the same time, do the people consider that legitimate? Was it their idea? Was it their solution? What we do consider successful in eradicating poppies was wheat, wheat seed. We were able to get huge quantities of wheat due to Agriculture folks. That was a big success. This stimulated the economy.

Some of the negatives in Afghanistan were:

- Road development did not work well. Afghanistan is a vast country with very difficult terrain and it is extremely hard to place roads where you cannot secure them.

- Education in the area was bad. It came down to money to build schools, pay teachers, etc., yet if the U.S. could not sustain the schools over a period of time then there is no point in building because you lose the confidence of the people. Your credibility will be lost on account of having to pull out from the area, thus abandoning the people.

- You can have the greatest idea in the world, but will you be able to put a local face on it? Their heart has to be in it, too. For example, our idea of policing and their idea of policing are not the same. The Afghan army supported the police in his area.

- Policing in this part of the world is more than making sure the petty criminal isn't taking things; these criminals are carrying AK-47s and APGs on their shoulders. The Army is very capable of dealing with this; from their perspective, they are the best Army they have had been in a while; the police force is coming along and is doing slightly better. The rule of law was an issue—we wanted to enforce it, but could not understand why criminals were released. Once we started talking to the judges, we understood that the official wanted payoffs because the tribal strategy was to "buy" the criminal out of jail in order to "reform" it; this has worked for centuries.

MR. VANGALA RAM

Mr. Vangala Ram, a Department of State FSO now attending Senior Training at ICAF, was our final speaker. He focused on his experiences as the Senior Civilian Representative (SCR) at RC–West in Herat, Afghanistan, for 16 months in 2007–08. The RC–West Command is dominated by Italian and Spanish forces, making communication an issue, at times. Mr. Ram focused some of his energy on the effective implementation of a wide range of State–INL programs. Since returning to the U.S., Mr. Ram has also volunteered to serve as a Senior Mentor and Subject Matter Expert (SME) for civilians who are now assigned to Afghanistan. He serves as a Mentor for the training they undergo at Camp Atterbury in Indiana. Concerning the INL programs, which were operated through a contractor (Dyncorp), Mr. Ram expressed some reservations regarding the lack of cultural awareness on the part of some personnel, hence the value of the new civilian training programs. Mr. Ram also highlighted his work at the major border crossing point with Iran, known as Musa Qala. He notified the audience of the extensive corruption evident there; where some 60% of the GOA revenue derives from. Mr. Ram also pointed out why and how his extensive liaison with the Afghan Border Police (ABP) regional commander was so critical in mitigating at least some of the evident corruption.

Mr. Ram performed a great deal of his effort on resolving areas of friction between INL and the U.S. military. The INL contractors were housed and co-located with the U.S. military in the region. Mr. Ram represented the USG in the region—as such, integrating our efforts with the

EU was also of critical importance. For example, he helped to integrate the work of the Italian Carbinieri with the efforts of the CIVPOL INL trainers for the ANSF—particularly the ANP. Finally, Mr. Ram has additional responsibilities for monitoring the extensive Iranian presence in western Afghanistan. He stressed the importance of coordination and avoiding duplication of effort as well as the importance of language and cultural awareness in this sensitive region of Afghanistan

SOME QUESTIONS TO THE PANEL

Some of the questions to the panel were:

Q: What was the experience with Afghan border police?

A: Afghan border police were found severely under-resourced; there was no accountability for weapons; they could never get a fix on what weapons were given to them; there was a lot of corruption at the border. A great deal depended on leadership.

Q: The justice system is questionable; there is no strategy. With all of these problems how can we have an effective policing system and how can we sustain a safe environment?

A: No strategy, no concept, no partner. They now have a combined ANA and ADP who are mutually supporting each other. The Partnering piece is key—the more the units were partnered the more effective they became, but still have to work on how personality-driven they were.

KEY FINDINGS

There are many lessons learned from the Iraq and Afghanistan operations. Those lessons can be summarized as follows:

1. *There are fundamental differences in overall COIN strategies between Iraq and Afghanistan.* In Iraq, the goal was and is to generate a democratic society; while in Afghanistan, the strategy continues to change. It ranged from removing the Taliban as government to providing security operations to developing an Afghan army to reconciliation. These changes in strategies made it difficult to prosecute a war with a moving endgame. The impact of this variation in strategies had a

significant impact on the guidance to the military and execution of COIN operations.

2. ***Building the capacity for the military to move within the population was critical.*** This freedom of action is important to engaging the population in defeating the insurgency. As General Petraeus said, "We have learned that the only way to secure the population is to live with it." This engagement of the population produced many successes but with a high increase in U.S. and Allied casualties.

3. ***There was no doctrine and the chain of command was not unified.*** There were a number of chains of command working in parallel and this made it difficult to identify the person in charge. In fact, there were the ISAF, GIRoA and DoS as the leading command authorities with multiple and sometimes intertwined chains that made it difficult to exercise proper authority and certainly added to the confusion at the lower levels of the chain.

4. ***Using a civil affairs team to partner with the police is critical to the operations.*** This partnership and sometimes mentoring resulted in a number of successful operations. However, one area of concern was when the police were of a different ethnic background than the local population. This led to a lack of trust and conflict. The Afghan border police were under resourced and lacked accountability. Corruption was widely spread.

5. ***There have been many opportunities to impose the U.S. and Allied procedures and processes.*** It is important to recognize that it is the Afghans' lives, their country, and it has to be the Afghans' solutions. The U.S. and Allies have to give them some tools that they can use, and then help with the execution and backup when needed.

6. ***There were many successes and failures.*** The ability to secure major roads and polling stations was considered a major success. Furthermore, one method of eradicating poppies was wheat (wheat seed). This resulted in stimulating the economy for the people. Not being able to sustain the schools that were built was considered a failure. Another failure was cultural awareness. For example, the rule of law was an issue and it was going to be enforced, but criminals were continually being

released. Thus officials had to be bribed since the tribal strategy was to "buy" the criminal out of jail in order to "reform" him.

7. ***There are connections between drug traffickers, terrorists, and insurgents.*** They received the money and protection they needed to move their products and the drugs were moved overseas. There needs to be an overall strategy that focuses on multiple provinces and not just one region otherwise the problem will never be solved.

There was general agreement that policing is important to counterinsurgency operations. However, the role of the police needs to be clearly defined. There are two approaches to policing in counterinsurgency. One is to use the police as a force multiplier; we run personnel through a short program, give them a badge, and send them out on the streets. The second is to look at the police as a force that builds relationships with community and protects them. The community will then provide information about insurgency. The debate will continue as to which approach is best in dealing with counterinsurgency. The lessons learned from the Iraq and Afghanistan operations highlighted in this Chapter can be instrumental in the assessment of the best approach toward policing in such environments. There are no templates for future conflicts, and as General Petraeus has stated, we have to protect the population first, then learn and adapt.

REFERENCES

1. Sewall, Sarah, John Nagl, David Petraeus, and James Amos, 2007. *The U.S. Army/Marine Corps Counterinsurgency Field Manual*, First Edition. Chicago: University of Chicago Press.

2. Kilcullen, David, 2010. *Counterinsurgency.* New York: Oxford University Press.

3. Nagl, John, 2005. *Learning to Eat Soup with a Knife: Counterinsurgency Lessons from Malaya and Vietnam*, First Edition. Chicago: University of Chicago Press.

4. Ricks, Thomas, 2009. *The Gamble: General David Petraeus and the American Military Adventure in Iraq, 2006–2008*. Penguin Press.

5. Roberts, M.E., 2005. *Villages of the Moon: Psychological Operations in Southern Afghanistan.* Publish America.

6. Marston, Daniel and Carter Malkasian, 2008. *Counterinsurgency in Modern Warfare.* Osprey Publishing.

7. Cassidy, Robert, 2006. *Counterinsurgency and the War on Terror.* Praeger Security International.

8. U.S. Government Counterinsurgency Guide, January 2009. Bureau of Political-Military Affairs.

9. General David Petraeus, memo on Counterinsurgency Guidance, July 2010.

10. Nagl, John, 2010. *World Politics Review*, October 18, 2010.

11. Secretary Robert Gates, 2010. Memorandum to Services.

12. Greek, E.E., 2010. "The Security Trinity," *Joint Force Quarterly* 59, 4th Quarter, 2010. Washington, DC: NDU Press.

13. Hagerott, M., T. Umberg, and J. Jackson, 2010. "Establishing the Rule of Law in Afghanistan," *Joint Force Quarterly* 59, 4th Quarter, 2010. Washington, DC.: NDU Press.

Chapter 6: Lessons Learned from Past Conflicts

Matt Keegan

Visiting Fellow, Center for Technology and National Security Policy
National Defense University, Fort McNair
and Chief of Staff and Vice President, U.S. Strategy
Selex Galileo, Inc., Arlington, Virginia

Matt Keegan, who is Visiting Fellow, Center for Technology and National Security Policy, National Defense University, Fort McNair, and Chief of Staff and Vice President, U.S. Strategy, Selex Galileo, Inc., Arlington, Virginia, chaired Roundtable VI: Lessons Learned from Past Conflicts. The first speaker for the session was Eric Beinhart, Senior Criminal Justice Advisor from the Department of Justice, on loan to USAID as part of the Rule of Law Team from the Democracy and Governance Office. Eric's presentation touched on key themes of the acceptable nature of the rule of law and the local nature of the effort and in its entirety represents a success at the Phase Zero level. The second speaker on the panel brought a global perspective to the group. Though retired, he was an extremely senior U.S. Government official with significant authority over U.S. Special Forces Command. As he remains active in the community today he requested that the author fully embrace the time-honored tradition at National Defense University of non-attribution. The last speaker on the panel was Colonel Bill Coultrup, U.S. Army. Colonel Coultrup had just returned from commanding the Joint Special Operations Task Force–Philippines (JSOTF–P). This force was composed of the local Foreign Internal Defense forces (FID) and civilian and military personnel from both U.S. and Philippine agencies, helping each other to overcome insurgent threats within the island nation.

INTRODUCTION

To quote the famous Spanish philosopher and novelist George Santayana "those who cannot remember the past are condemned to repeat it."[1] The past experiences in counterinsurgency (COIN) of success such as Malaya and India, or defeats such as Vietnam offer lessons and methods that should be remembered and can be applied or avoided in order to achieve a positive outcome in today's COIN operations. Chapter 5 reviewed the war fighter deliberations of our current engagements in Iraq and Afghanistan, so to follow, this chapter will look at other recent successes that have occurred over roughly the last decade both large and small to hopefully glean methods or lessons for success.

The "Lessons Learned" Panel was composed of three leaders who had personally engaged in various counterinsurgency efforts ranging from Phase Zero Stability–type "Prevent or Prepare" activities, to Phase Four "Establish Security" and Phase Five operations aimed at returning nations back to "Civil Authority" and Rule of Law.[2] The speakers offered evidence over the course of the deliberations that police and military both had roles that, though they overlap in the COIN operations, point to the police being the key in the final establishment and maintenance of stability. What appears to be the underlying theme is that to achieve and maintain stability within a nation-state it is essential that the government be able to establish and maintain the Rule of Law. Depending on the degree of instability, this will require varied degrees of military and paramilitary force to establish basic security. Sustainable and persistent security requires a transition to an acceptable Rule of Law at the local level, which is maintained by a credible local police force, or risk being doomed to failure.

This author would offer that to defeat an insurgency is as much, if not more political activity in nature than military. From a military practitioner's mindset this is evidenced by an author whose primary work rests on the shelves of every War College graduate, Carl Von Clausewitz. Clausewitz plainly states in his text *On War* that war is "a true political instrument, a continuation of political intercourse, carried on by other means."[3] Connecting Clausewitz with DOD's Joint Publication (JP) 3–24 and its definition of insurgency being a form of irregular warfare, allows the simple connection that insurgency is a form of politics.[4] This plainly supports JP 3–24 with the quote that opens Chapter II, "Insurgency," from Anthony James Jones that states, "The beginning of wisdom is to grasp and hold on tightly to the idea that insurgency is a profoundly political problem."[5] To further extend this tenet, a quote from former Speaker of the House Tip O'Neill (which he had borrowed from his father), one that every Capitol Hill politician is always reminded of as election season approaches, is that "all politics is local."[5] Combining the thoughts of Clausewitz, JP 3–24, Mr. Jones, and Speaker O'Neill leads one to "all insurgency warfare is an extension of local politics." To complete the connection, this is "the beginning of wisdom," which becomes the first step and key underlying lesson in how to defeat an insurgency. Not only is this theory supported by the experiences of the Panel, but also finds solid support from General

Petraeus's counterinsurgency guidance of July 2010, where he outlines how to secure, serve, live with, and build relationships with the local population. In General Petraeus's own words, "We have to put our forces, together with those of our coalition partners and our host nation counterparts, in neighborhoods whose occupants we are striving to secure."

To paraphrase David Kilcullen and the thinking he offers in his book, *The Accidental Guerrilla*, insurgency is a race between a determined insurgent element and the government with the goal being popular support and "influence and control at a grassroots level."[6] This requires the insurgent force to overcome the government (and its politics) and the Rule of Law within a region. Whether rooted in ideology, criminal intent, or in the pursuit of pure power, an insurgency must gain its "support" from the populace before the government can quell the uprising by eliminating safe heavens, capturing or killing its leadership, shutting down its financial/economic support, and/or countering and discrediting its message and thereby eliminating the necessary popular support. Insurgency must therefore rapidly establish itself among the local populace from which it recruits its resources, finds its safe havens, and grows its strength.

Two recent examples support the need to defeat insurgents at the local level and "by, with and through" supporting the local population. First is the original defeat of the FARC in Colombia. Plan Colombia reflects this sort of thinking by President Uribe and his administration. Though he received American training, technical assistance, and aid dollars, the actions were applied by the Colombian Military and National Police, which "successfully diminished the threat of insurgency to the country's political stability."[7] Plan Colombia, a counterinsurgency plan of Colombian design, aimed to "improve security in Colombia by re-claiming control over areas held by the illegal armed groups."[8] The heart of the plan was a whole-of-government approach which applied the national military and police to reestablish security in contested regions and then rapidly provided aid and assistance to the local "freed" communities that enabled them to "reenter viable civic and economic life." Although narcotics trafficking is still a dominant force within Colombia, the threat to governmental stability was eliminated over a 5-year period.[8]

Second, is an example from combat operations in Al Anbar Province in Iraq. The region was one of the most violent regions in Iraq, where the insurgents based much of their activity in the days following the fall of Baghdad to Coalition Forces in 2003. Lieutenant Colonel James Giles Kyser, United States Marine Corps, was the Commander of the 2 Battalion, 2 Marines in Anbar. Col. Kyser noted when interviewed that the most effective method of eliminating the insurgency was town-by-town and by working with the locals to reestablish control of their villages. The Marines would work within the local culture to reinforce (or establish) stability and reinvigorate the local Rule of Law. This Rule of Law was not necessarily the same as the law of the land, but the law with which the local community was most comfortable and had the longest established history. Such law could have been religion-based like Muslim Sharia law, tribally based, or civil based, depending on the village. Through security (often kinetic) actions/operations, combined with humanitarian aid and economic assistance, the USMC changed Anbar from an insurgent safe haven into an area where Al Qa'ida terrorist and/or anti-government insurgent forces were no longer welcome, and in several instances they were actually chased from towns by the locals themselves.

Both examples demonstrate, and the panelists' deliberations that follow will support, that in order to defeat an insurgency one must create an environment of stability, reestablish accepted local Rule of Law, and do so in a way that is credible, acceptable and therefore persistent. Though foreign support may be necessary to establish (or re-establish) the security, in the end it must be maintained by the locals. Depending on the degree of stability within the region and the perceived ability (and need) of a foreign military to address the instability, there is a line, in some places thin, between establishing security and stable, accepted Rule of Law, and foreign occupation with levied law. When foreign forces are used, or military forces applied to establish stability, it must be done so with knowledge that transition to local police forces is essential to success. Otherwise, there is a risk of being viewed as an occupier or oppressor which only creates a fertile field for the growth of the insurgency it is trying to defeat.

Persistence of Rule of Law is also a critical element that only local law enforcement/police can establish. Military forces are transitional by design, both economically and politically unsupportable over a longer period of time in both an international and local sense. Local police composed of native personnel and who have grown up in the cultural and social fabric of the region can embody the persistent Rule of Law that will keep stability. Again, there is an element of politics and balance. Police who are seen as corrupt or tied to a corrupt or illegitimate government may become a motivating factor in an insurgency, but conversely, when seen as the legitimate and persistent arm of the government, it is more frequently welcomed. With the support of the populace, police can protect citizens while respecting their human rights and dignity and keep peace at the local level. The experience of the first panel member and his work in Northern Uganda works to demonstrate how the enhancement of a local police force and acceptable Rule of Law has worked to keep and enhance stability in the region.

PANEL DELIBERATIONS

The first speaker for the session was Eric Beinhart, Associate Director of the Department of Justice's International Criminal Investigative Training Assistance Program (DOJ/ICITAP), who is serving on a three-year detail to USAID's Office of Democracy and Governance as a Senior Criminal Justice Advisor. Eric's presentation touched on key themes of the acceptable nature of the Rule of Law and the local nature of the effort, and in its entirety, represents a success at the Phase Zero level. This success was achieved through the application of a whole-of-government effort ranging from the U.S. Army to the United Nations with the specific program designed by DOJ/ICITAP and USAID. The program itself was aimed at reestablishing a statuary legal system in Northern Uganda as well as a juvenile justice system, in order to provide the local populace with a Rule of Law that functioned across the spectrum of legal activity . . . from daily police enforcement through the court system . . . making this a fully functional system based in the socio-cultural roots of the region and accomplished by local officials. This local commitment helped establish a credible, acceptable, local method of maintaining regional stability. It also helped mitigate the risk of instability in a nation with a history of insurgency, government overthrows, and disenfranchised populace/political elements taking up arms against the established authority.

To understand the environment that drove the need for these efforts and in which the whole-of-government team had to operate, Eric offered that a note of "Ugandan history must be cited to put information in context." Milton Obote was the first Prime Minister (later President) of Uganda after independence from Great Britain was established in 1962. Obote was overthrown by Idi Amin in 1971, and Amin was in turn overthrown by the Tanzanian Army in 1979 after he unsuccessfully tried to invade Tanzania. Obote returned as president in 1981. Idi Amin is widely held up as an example of a brutal dictator who nearly destroyed his country through his own excesses. "Obote, however, was no prize either, as his leadership contributed to widespread destabilization of Uganda." In 1985, with constant pressure being applied from an ever strengthening National Resistance Army (NRA) in the north—led by Yoweri Museveni—Obote fled into exile. Gen. Basilio Olara-Okello briefly served as president but he fled into exile in January 1986 when the NRA consolidated its power. Museveni formed a government and has served as Uganda's president ever since.

The Acholi people of Uganda—Okello's ethnic group—did not take the stand up of the Museveni Government well and to this day are still angry about the overthrow of General Okello. This anger, combined with underlying religious tension, has led to an ongoing insurrection and the creation of the Lord's Resistance Army (LRA) in 1987, which wreaked havoc in the country until 2006. Northern Uganda suffered through nearly constant turbulence, conflict and insurgency.

With the history established, Eric then offered the context against which the program was specifically targeted.

- From 1986–2006 there was no statuary legal system in Northern Uganda. Customary law was in place, and local councils were set up by President Museveni that became the municipal government. The hierarchy roughly had village leaders going up to local councils, and beyond that there were country districts divided down to the county, sub-county, and village levels.

- The program was more than an effort to enhance community policing, it focused on reestablishing a functioning legal system in Lira Town, located within the Lira District. It made no sense to focus just on the police if nothing else worked in terms of the legal system. The program had to focus not only on supporting and developing a local police force and its capabilities, but on the connection and functioning of the courts system as well in order to create a functioning, credible legal system and credible Rule of Law that could take a crime from investigation through prosecution.

- The team could test methodologies to see how things worked as they were functioning in an area of relative stability [as opposed to other regions of Uganda or places like Iraq or Afghanistan].

- Lira District in Northern Uganda has a magisterial court, a police headquarters, prosecutor's office, and court building all centrally located in Lira Town, but there was poor coordination between these criminal justice actors.

This is a complicated issue, as the basis for Rule of Law in its local definition was deeply rooted in the society and operated in a more traditions-based fashion than what a western democracy would call a justice system. Eric offered an example from Northern Uganda; if there was a charge of rape in the village the elder of that village would handle it; the alleged perpetrator's family got together with the victim's family and they would work something out—whether it was the handing over of livestock, money, resources, etc., by the offender to the victim's family. This is a way it has been done for thousands of years. Then we arrive and start talking about a western statutory legal system when there hasn't been one in force for 20 some years. In 2007, we were talking to the detectives, and they said that someone would make a rape charge against another community member, but that is done as a threat in the continuing negotiation over the settlement, not as something that the victim's family actually wants to prosecute, but as a method of obtaining payment. If a settlement is reached, a criminal case is withdrawn, and as statutory rape was a capital offense, this was the preferred way of ending the dispute. Some parents would "game" the system, making false charges or setting up crimes in order to gain settlements. For example, they would offer their daughters to men and later claim that the young women were less than 16 years of age, the legal age of consent in Northern Uganda, and pursue charges of rape. If a settlement was reached before the case was brought before the courts the family would drop the charges and thus achieve their objective of receiving some sort of fairly significant payment through this "gaming." There was a big backlog of cases like this with no real way to verify the age of the people because the vital records systems was dysfunctional.

The program started after an assessment in March of 2007. From the beginning, the program faced a large obstacle in that the funding would expire and revert to the U.S. Treasury on October 1, 2007. This only allowed 4.5 months to implement a very serious and ambitious program. Where bad fortune had struck them at the budget level, good fortune had come in the form of two experienced teams. "We were fortunate to have really experienced people who advised police and prosecutors, and who had international experience in places like Bosnia and other sub-Saharan African countries," said Beinhart. So, with only 4.5 months of funding the two teams had to execute the ambitious program of melding a community policing with community prosecution into a coordinated, cohesive system where no system had existed for decades prior.

As a first step in implementing the program, the first team's lead advisors gathered the police, prosecutors, magistrate, senior advisors, United Nations Development Program (UNDP) officials, United Nations High Commissioner for Human Rights officials, U.S. Army Civil Affairs officers and others together to discuss problems in the criminal justice system. Together they focused on a case that had already been adjudicated—the rape of a 6-year-old girl—and then talked about it among themselves trying to understand the failures of the case. Initially, there was normal finger-pointing, but after a few hours they got beyond the competition and appointing of blame between departments. They agreed that the local police were doing a lot of things right, but they looked at ways where things could be improved in terms of conducting witness interviews, pre-documentation, forensic analysis, etc. This went on for several weeks, working closely with the detective units from Lyerla and looking at the developing the institution.

Eric continued that it is important to note that this was not training, but mentoring. His team brought the groups together and worked alongside of the local officers and officials not trying to establish a form of justice that was foreign to the region (such as an American model), but looking at the institutions and how the local authorities by working together could improve the system from within.

Over the next few months the team, together with the local police and justice officials, undertook multiple efforts aimed at reestablishing a credible Rule of Law in the region. Example activities included:

- Uganda police were hiring special constables who had no official training. The U.S. Team worked with the police, prosecutors and the magistrate to develop a curriculum which focused on very basic things: interview/ interrogation, report writing, etc. and helped establish a connected and coherent method for investigation, case development and recording, and associated prosecution.

- US Army Civil Affairs unit medics worked with DOJ/ICITAP instructors to prepare first aid training for the local police. This proved to be particularly effective in teaching simple, practical things that the police could use to help build trust and relationships with the people and to significantly enhance their acceptance, support, and creditability in the local community.

- DOJ/ICITAP worked with police, prosecutors, a magistrate, and UN officials to develop a course entitled, "Building the Capacity of Police Constables within a Community Policing Framework." In order to optimize time and money the course was developed to teach 22 local instructors, who in turn trained 200 other officers.

- The Chief of Police, the State Prosecutor, and the Chief Magistrate signed a Memorandum of Understanding in which the three offices pledged to work together more effectively. The DOJ/ICITAP police and prosecutorial advisors worked with their Ugandan counterparts to institute "Roll Call Training" that stress 20 minutes of training several times a week on important topics. When the State Prosecutor in Lira was reassigned to another district, he immediately instituted this training approach with the police.

- There was no juvenile justice system in Uganda. With ICITAP's assistance, the Chief of Police, the State Prosecutor, the Chief Magistrate, and Catholic priests agreed on an experimental juvenile justice initiative that was to be overlooked by priests. The priests agreed to supervise the work of juvenile offenders—this became the model throughout other areas of Uganda. This is an interesting note as it did two things; handled the youth in a more custom-based fashion while minimizing the strain on the justice system itself. In the end, it is keeping the youth out of the penal system that could do more to make them disenfranchised.

- The last step was with infrastructure improvement. USAID/ICITAP provided $25,000 in refurbishments to the Lira Police Headquarters that included: roof repairs, the installation of internal electrical wiring (outlets, etc.) throughout the facility, painting, plastering, and other structural repairs, door, and window repairs, the installation of mosquito netting for windows and vents, plumbing repairs, and main gate repairs. This was done at the end of the program after all stakeholders bought into the institutional development focus of the program. Police felt pride in their new station and citizens expressed satisfaction in visiting a clean, professional building to report crimes.

Unfortunately it was a rushed program, but it offers some valuable lessons learned in terms of how institutional development can best be promoted in the criminal justice sector. Most importantly, this model can be replicated not just within Uganda but in other parts of the world. The entire program was a grass-roots, "boot-strapped" effort. It brought local actors together, worked within their traditional social and cultural values, and was facilitated through USG and international donor sources acting in a mentoring capacity. The program helped guide Ugandan government agencies through a process of institutional development that included technical assistance and training, but by allowing Ugandans to lead, it never violated the basic regional tenets or in any way gave the appearance of a foreign system being levied on a local system. The local community took ownership quickly and with a guiding hand from experienced professionals was able to more effectively establish the Rule of Law and enhance the stability of Northern Uganda.

The second speaker on the panel brought a global perspective to the group. Though retired, he was an extremely senior U.S. Government official with significant authority over U.S. Special Forces Command. As he remains active in the community today he requested that the author fully embrace the time honored tradition at National Defense University of non-attribution. He spoke to the group more from the perspective of a counterinsurgency war fighter with a view that COIN success requires long-term commitment, absolute local commitment, a whole-of-government approach, and the establishment of locally acceptable Rule of Law.

The SOCOM speaker opened his presentation with a basic truth not only about COIN, but also placed it in the context of the "hearts and minds" of the American "voting" public. He cited the writings of David Kilcullen, who said it takes 15–20 years to resolve an insurgency. This fact in and of itself presents a daunting commitment of military and economic resources. It means carrying a coherent strategy through a minimum of four Presidential elections. With that in mind he suggested that this timeframe be compared with the patience of American people when they hear this timeframe and compare it to the potential loss of "American treasure," including both the lives of young men and women and dollars being redirected from an ailing economy. The result is a dramatic imbalance proven over the history of American participation in foreign wars. The unfortunate logic behind that time period vs. patience mismatch is something that works to the disadvantage of the American strategy when the necessary patience and long-term commitment is not there to maintain the resolve. This creates unrealistic timelines and the need to more rapidly establish local military, paramilitary and law enforcement forces capable of establishing and maintaining the necessary Rule of Law, which is a central objective in defeating any insurgency.

The term "defeat" then becomes an interesting point for discussion. In order to "defeat" a COIN adversary you need to understand the local socio-cultural and political dynamics of the environment in which the battle is being waged. Our speaker's many years in combating insurgency warfare directly echoes General Petraeus's words and supports the idea that the defeat of an insurgency can only be accomplished by those who live within its fabric, who understand acceptable and pre-established norms, the local definition of Rule of Law (as opposed to a form of Western law, which can be very foreign to a distant culture and therefore disenfranchising), and the connections to the society. Such an understanding is essential and can only be developed either by having grown up in the society or spending many years in it. Short rotations of young men and women, which is a basic tenet in the organizational culture of the American military, is diametrically opposed to this sort of long-term assimilation of the local socio-cultural fabric. Without this developed understanding it is nearly impossible to defeat a COIN enemy or create sustainable conditions to achieve a solution in the long term. The history of COIN warfare notes that even when fighting in the long-term or short-term, as much as eighty percent of insurgencies are resolved in favor of the government, but usually through an arrangement between insurgents and governments.

This was supported in a RAND study issued early this year [2010] entitled *How Insurgencies End*, by Ben Connable and Martin Libicki. Such a negotiated settlement . . . as opposed to "defeat" . . . requires a complete understanding of the socio-cultural element, but also leaves basic and extremist elements of the insurgency within the society. If a popularly supported Rule of Law and the associate credible and accepted law enforcement authority is not put in place over the course of the counterinsurgent fight (and negotiation), the radical elements can use any unpopular element of the Rule of Law against the Government and over a period of time begin the cycle again as a resurgent force. Such is the case in Peru where increased narcotics production is funding the now resurgent Shining Path. In sum, complete defeat most probably is an unrealistic objective, while a functional arrangement has proven to be historically realistic.

It is certainly worthwhile to note that long-term does not necessarily end with the cessation of hostilities. In order to maintain the "concluded balance" within a society, rebuilding a war-torn nation must be completed or risk the growth of local anger against the government and recreating the fertile environment for the extremist insurgence to rebuild (local) popular anti-government. These rebuilding efforts are evident as we are trying to come out with stability in Iraq and Afghanistan. It takes years to establish new infrastructures, teach local nationals how to maintain them, and stand up a local Rule of Law that is acceptable and locally supported. Additionally, studies indicate that Security, Stabilization, Transition, and Reconstruction (SSTR) operations can take five times the economic commitment to rebuild a region as it did for the war to tear it down. Our speaker noted that in Iraq we are drawing down our forces, but some of our people like Special Operators are there for the long term as they promote stability through the rebuilding of the society for many years to come (e.g., Civil Affairs units, Engineering and Construction teams, training forces, etc.).

As a COIN fight is one that requires adversaries and government alike to gain or maintain popular support, a sustainable conclusion cannot be achieved solely through the application of military force. The true targets are the "hearts and minds" of the populace and trying to create a peaceful, safe, and sustainable environment. Traditional military units are not built to accomplish this task, nor are the Special Operations Forces, who can affect varying degrees of training of locals and the rebuilding of infrastructure (e.g., roads, rail, public works) and other "hearts and minds" operations, but do not have the complete expertise of the many other economic, development (e.g., farming, inter-region commerce, banking), and governing elements brought to bear by other agencies who are better prepared to achieve this objective. Evidence of this was offered by Eric Beinhart when he demonstrated the effective role of the Department of Justice and USAID as well as NGOs and the UNDP and UNHCHR. Further evidence can be witnessed when looking at Plan Colombia, where military forces gave way to police and police maintained the peace while economically focused government elements helped the locals revitalize the economy.[10] Our speaker offered his first-hand experience in Kosovo, where he noted that the rebuilding of such things as schools and clinics went a long way to winning the hearts and minds of the people and therefore was extremely important and effective (he also noted that most of this effort was done by the Civil Affairs units from the U.S. Reserves forces). In other instances such as the efforts in Southeast Asia, "medical (and veterinarian) capabilities were very important for a lot of these people because a water buffalo might be their most important possession, as it was essential to sustain not just their economic livelihood, but their very survival!"

"Anything you can do to first understand the people and what's important to them and then get into the hearts and minds of the people you are with is essential in establishing the necessary foundation for successfully ending an insurgency." The only way to go forward in bringing an insurgency to an acceptable end is to proceed with a whole-of- government approach. As our speaker offered, "look at an operation and the society in which it operates and come up with the center of gravity and go for it. In today's world everyone is dependent upon each other for a solution—it's all about joint, combined, interagency efforts. This really becomes a success if it works. In Thailand, U.S. Forces took the Ambassador to see our Special Operators at work. They were not breaking down doors or shooting the bad guys, they were doing medical work throughout the community. Ninety percent of what Special Operations Forces do is winning the minds and hearts of the people in the country in which they are located; it's all about relationships you build in the countries where you work. The key is the whole-of-government (police, NGOs, etc.) and how to bring them all together for a solution. When a solution is established 'by, with, and through' the local society it will be accepted and therefore will stand the test of time. You need to leave behind a structure that will be resilient and withstand adverse conditions or risk returning to fight the same enemies again."

Resilience goes hand in hand with acceptable Rule of Law. This Rule of Law must be acceptable to those it governs or it risks alienating the very population it is designed to serve. What it is frequently not acceptable is a system of law levied by a foreign authority based on foreign cultural norms as opposed to local socio-cultural norms. The time tested traditions of bartered justice in Africa or religious-based law used in many Muslim nations are just two examples of legal systems that would be unacceptable in a system based on western legal traditions. It is, however, historically and culturally entrenched, and therefore acceptable, in many societies around the world. Our speaker offered the example where U.S. Forces supported the capture of a leading terrorist in Southeast Asia. U.S. Forces wanted to bring the person to justice through due process, but "the locals did not see it that way. The local solution had a much more immediate and definite end for our former terrorist and that was and is a societal norm for the region. No matter how we look at the rule of law, other people have different interpretations." If U.S. Forces had attempted to overcome the local Rule of Law by forcing American norms on a non-American society, we would have violated acceptable local tenets creating friction and dissension, which would have been counterproductive to our long-term security goals in the region.

The final part of the SOCOM presenter's discussions focused on the establishment or maintenance of the Rule of Law as a central element of an SSTR operation. Whether sustaining Phase Zero stability or returning to stability from conflict in Phases Four or Five, having a Rule of Law maintained by the locals, accepted in method, recognized as fair (which is certainly relative to the society and culture) and maintained by a police force as opposed to a military is a basic building block. It is important to differentiate the use of forces for two reasons; (1) the purpose and skills of the forces applied and the appropriateness of the role, and (2) the perception by the populace of fair and acceptable rather than occupier or oppressor.

To the first point, general-purpose military forces are designed for short-term, high energy, and kinetic effect. American forces have never been designed as occupying forces nor would the American people stand for it. They are designed for forced entry and sustained combat operations. Yes, there are elements within the force such as military police, civil affairs units, engineering units, etc., but they are designed as part of the operational element of supporting combat operations and the transition of operations from combat to reconstruction and sustained peace. Conversely, police forces are frequently recruited and operated locally, have a protective role for the people they serve, have limited kinetic capability, and are built to deter. They are part of the fabric of society they protect and gain strength through their connection with the local population. They protect it from violations of law that represent temporary flashes of instability and help sustain a justice system that holds the society together. Time and experience have proven that military and police forces have clear, distinct roles. Although they often have a shared gray area of transition, they are distinct from each other. Military forces can defeat an opposing force and start a nation back down the road to Rule of Law but without a fair, accepted local police force and criminal justice system, the sustainability of the peace is impossible. A nation that tries to use military forces in a police role will only transmit a heavy-handed message of occupation that frequently promotes future insurgence. Similarly, a police force is ill-equipped or trained to execute sustained military action, but is essential when a population is returned to everyday life.

Our Special Operator then offered a model for future COIN operations, the Joint Special Operations Task Force–Philippines (JSOTF–P). This operation clearly depicts the long-term commitment, absolute local commitment, a whole-of-government approach, and established/maintained locally acceptable Rule of Law necessary to overcome an insurgency. Conducted side-by-side by U.S. and Philippine forces and agencies, the Task Force has been successful in eliminating multiple threats to the stability of the Philippine government through the application of local forces/agencies with U.S. support and reflects the methods and thinking the U.S. will have to bring to various regions to keep the world a safer place.

Our SOCOM speaker's last words for the day acted as a perfect transition to the last speaker on the panel, Colonel Bill Coultrup, U.S. Army. Col. Coultrup had just returned from commanding the JSOTF–P. This force was composed of the local Foreign Internal Defense forces (FID) and civilian and military personnel from both U.S. and Philippine agencies helping each other to overcome insurgent threats within the island nation. Col. Coultrup's presentation demonstrated how many of the key tenets discussed by our prior speakers can be brought together in a whole-of-government (military, police, civilian agencies, NGOs, etc.) effort supported by and supporting the local Rule of Law and even in the face of funding constraints (a similar hurdle to the one overcome by Mr. Beinhart's teams in Uganda) to achieve success.

Col. Coultrup opened his discussion by outlining the resources and objectives of the JSOTF–P. This Task Force, in coordination with the U.S. country team, conducted internal defense activities with the Republic of the Philippines Security Forces in order to defeat Jamal-i-Islamiya (JI) and Abu Sayyaf (AS), arrest high value individuals and neutralize enemy safe havens. From a U.S. Country Team perspective this meant supporting, training, and equipping while leaving any kinetic or enforcement actions to the local forces. While focused on JI and AS, the Task Force had to also consider other foreign influences in the Philippines such as the communists, rogue elements of Moro Liberation Front, and other elements of Islamic fronts. It is also important to note the Philippines is composed of a littoral geography and largely jungle-based ecosystem. In total these combined factors and threats stretches the Philippine military forces extremely thin and therefore requires options on how and who will react to the threat—it could be military or police depending on where, when and what. To meet this challenge the Task Force had up to 600 people in country, partnering with the Armed Forces of the Philippines (AFP) and the Philippines National Police (PNP) stressing training in basic officer policing, investigations, human rights, explosive ordnance disposal (note there was a significant focus on counter-IED training), civil military operations (infrastructure, medical and educational projects), and many other disciplines.

As part of the whole-of-government equation the Task Force worked very closely with ICITAP who focused on the basic officer training in the northern Philippines. In some areas, sixty percent of police personnel live below the poverty level and they have to buy their own weapons. ICITAP worked with the local government to train the police in basic police officer skills. The Federal Bureau of Investigation also provided two agents to work with both Philippine military and civil police. When the program ran out of money Task Force leadership brought in U.S. Military Police (MP) from Okinawa and had the MPs training the student officers in basic police skills like investigations and proper evidence collection. One other complication in utilizing the ICITAP trainers was getting them to the south of the country due to threat-driven embassy restrictions. For this reason, the Task Force had to facilitate getting other Task Force partners to the conflict areas to carry out missions such as police training as well as information operations, information gathering and sharing, civil-military engagement, and capacity-building. Because the ICITAP team was restricted from working in the south, this role was filled by the U.S. Navy SEALs who worked with their Philippine counterparts on a daily basis.

Rule of Law related efforts did not just stop at training at the officer level. The Task Force also worked with the prosecutor's office. The Philippine justice system has strict rules as it pertains to obtaining a warrant to go after individuals which is out of balance with the time sensitive nature of the pursuit of the high value individuals in question. The team, working within the local process, engaged with local prosecutors and judges to develop a method of presenting them with evidence packages to get the warrants issued within a shorter time frame, thus allowing the military and police to go after suspects in a timely and legal fashion.

Other work with the judges and magistrates included improving their interaction with the AFP and the Philippine Coast Guard. This expanded the reach of the Rule of Law further into the island nation well beyond its original boundaries, which were heavily dictated by the ecosystem and geography. The coordination permitted the legal reach to extend beyond the road networks on the larger islands to those islands where separation by water also meant separation from the Rule of Law.

One of the most significant elements of the program was the Civil-Military Operations (CMO) component. This demonstrated to the locals that there was a better way to sustain their well-being and that their Government was able to help them realize it. CMOs helped in building schools, making bridges to be able to cross rivers, expanding infrastructure, and offering medical services. Operations like these not only opened inter-city commerce, but also permitted the Task Force to conduct educational Civil Action Programs. Programs like these brought the police and AFP officials face-to-face with the public, enabling them to build trusting relationships with villages and townspeople where distrust or limited trust may have existed before.

CMO also helped to reduce safe havens for the insurgents. For example, a proposed dirt road project would be offered and coordinated with everyone in the region. Word would quickly spread to the insurgents who would then say "we need to move. The military (Americans) are building roads and this will give AFP speed of attack. This is going to make life hard and our people will not support us anymore." A very simple project like a dirt road would therefore bring with it enhanced security, but would also yield the positive secondary effect of promoting and/or increasing commerce between local villages to towns, thereby enhancing the economic well-being of the residents. In total, one road would equate to two "positive effect points" for the government and against the insurgents.

A similar simple security-enhancing project was the opening of an emergency call center. Until this time there was no U.S. "911"-like center, leaving the locals with no way of rapidly interacting with local police. This shortcoming was rapidly overcome by a joint interagency effort. Now, not only can the public access emergency help, but the police and military can better help one another. This enhanced public-government support communications has enhanced public safety while decreasing the insurgents' freedom of movement. Initially, there was resistance from local police who did not want the military to see what kind of corruption was going on in the region, but in short course, the benefits outweighed the concern and the Center is up and running.

Much if not all of the JSOTF–P efforts were conducted with a whole-of-government, heavily interagency dependent methodology. At various points across the effort the Task Force itself had ten members and the Country Team another eight members. These groups where complemented by as many as another dozen partnerships with Philippine military and civil agencies as well as NGOs and PVOs. In total the available skill sets ranged from military and police to doctors, engineers and chaplains coming from organizations that span the spectrum of government and governmental support, such as the Peace Corps, the Red Cross, the Departments of Agriculture and Justice, Public Affairs units, and USAID. Many local institutions also contributed. For example, when the Task Force could not work directly with USAID it worked with local institutions in order to induce people to give up weapons in exchange for something else, like land. In total, it represented a true whole-of-government/interagency effort. It is worth noting though, that the interagency process is slow because there is not enough money to take on a multitude of projects while U.S. efforts in Afghanistan and Iraq are the major focus. In spite of this major limitation, however, this program demonstrates that success is possible.

At the close of his presentation Col. Coultrup offered several "take-aways" that he believes underlie the success of the JSOTF–Ps efforts and might be worthy consideration when designing future COIN strategies:

1. We [the U.S.] are not in charge (nor do we want to be). We are supporting the government of the Philippines and its Security Forces. We accomplish the U.S. strategic objectives *through, by and with* the Security Forces of the host nation.

2. Value long-term success over short-term gains.

3. Success requires synchronized interagency and whole-of-government efforts.

4. The government of the Philippines is changing the conditions that give rise to terrorism. They are enhancing good governance, the professionalism of their military [and police], and economic development across their nation.

5. When it comes to "needs vs. wants," limited resources dictate that we must focus on key areas. We cannot dictate what these areas are as it requires local "buy in" from local leadership, the community, and the security forces demonstrating the necessary degree of acceptance and commitment that is essential for success.

At the conclusion of Col. Coultrup's presentation, a member of the audience offered an interesting question which actually brings this Chapter full circle to its opening quote from Santayana. The participant asked, "There are a variety of organizations involved in peace operations. Have you got a system across the government to document the lessons learned?" "No, is the short answer," replied a panelist, "there are examples where we have captured such lessons, but not much more. Unfortunately, in the last seven years the bureaucratic turf battles between the Departments of State and Justice have made interagency collaboration increasingly difficult. There are case studies out there, but in terms of the U.S. Government, no. Time and time again, it's "old lessons re-learned."

KEY FINDINGS

The intent of this panel was to look back at recent operations and offer lessons learned so we don't repeat the mistakes of history or have to re-learn old lessons. The following is an effort to summarize the key points and contribute to the necessary documentation that can keep COIN efforts progressing:

1. ***Rule of Law is a keystone of stability***. It must be seen as long term and persistent in order to have credibility. Rule of Law must stem from acceptable, traditional and historic socio-cultural norms of the local region and not non-local practices from foreign sources.

2. *Campaigns must be whole-of-government interagency efforts in order to succeed.* Success requires working, training and mentoring the local populations to better their standard of living as opposed to a foreign system being levied by a perceived occupation force, a role frequently associated with military forces.

3. *Security in the form of military forces may have a role in either kinetic operations, training, and/or Civil Military Operations, but certainly police forces have an essential role in local, acceptable sustainment of security through local Rule of Law.* The perception (or reality) of heavy-handed military operations works against the success of COIN operations. The military role is key to establishing stability, but transition to police is equally essential to lasting peace and reducing the prospects re-insurgent efforts.

4. *Value of Civil-Military Operations should not be underestimated.* Within COIN Operations CMOs have proven to be a positive method of lowering public barriers and enhancing acceptance of government leadership. CMOs carry with them positive messages of support to the local populace and their economy.

5. *Whether military, CMO or police operations, the operating force must understand the socio-cultural norms of the region or risk alienating the populace and creating fertile fields for ongoing or future insurgency.*

6. *As "all insurgency is local," it is the locals who must "buy in" and actively participate in establishing stability in their nation.* Insurgency cannot be won by a perceived occupying force, it can only be won by, with and through the locals.

7. *Long-term success versus short-term gain holds the real value in establishing persistent stability within a region.*

REFERENCES

1. Wikipedia.org/George_Santayana.

2. Department of Defense Joint Publication 3–0, *Joint Operations*, 17 September 2006. Incorporating Changes 2, 22 March 2010, IV–27.

3. Clausewitz, Carl Von, 1989. *On War*. Princeton: Princeton University Press, 87.

4. Department of Defense Joint Publication 3–24, *Counterinsurgency Operations*, 5 October 2009.

5. O'Neill, Jr., Thomas P, 1987. *Man of the House: The Life and Political Memoirs of the Speaker Tip O'Neill*. New York: Random House.

6. Kilcullen, David, 2009. *The Accidental Guerrilla, Fighting Small Wars in the Midst of a Big One*. New York: Oxford University Press, xv.

7. Killebrew, Bob and Jennifer Beral, 2010. *Crime Wars, Gangs, Cartels and U.S. National Security*. Washington, DC: Center for New American Studies, 23.

8. Ibid.

9. Ibid.

10. Ibid.

11. O'Neill, Jr., Thomas P., 1987. *Man of the House*.

12. Kilcullen, David, 2009. *The Accidental Guerrilla*.

13. Killebrew, Bob and Jennifer Beral, 2010. *Crime Wars*.

14. Ibid.

15. Ibid.

16. Ibid.

Chapter 7: COIN Policy and Process

James M. Keagle

Director, Transforming National Security Seminar Series
Center for Technology and National Security Policy
National Defense University

Christopher Mann

Research Associate
Center for Technology and National Security Policy
National Defense University

"The Afghan government has not integrated or supported traditional community governance structures, historically an important component of Afghan civil society, leaving communities vulnerable to being undermined by insurgent groups and power-brokers."
General McChrystal, August 2009

Dr. James M. Keagle, the Director of the Transforming National Security seminar series at the Center for Technology and National Security Policy, National Defense University, chaired the Roundtable: COIN Policy and Process. Joseph Keefe, a Research Staff Member for the Institute of Defense Analyses, discussed the Focused District Development Concept (FDD). The aim of this six-phase program was initially to reform and professionalize local police units. T.X. Hammes, a Senior Research Fellow at the Institute for National Strategic Studies, National Defense University, argued that a successful COIN campaign must be police-led, intelligence-driven, and population-centric. Dr. Stephen Metz, currently the Chairman of the Regional Strategy and Planning Department at the U.S. Army War College Strategic Studies Institute, posited that the central problem is we tried to polish and apply 20th-century insurgency principles to 21st-century conflicts that differ in fundamental ways. Ms. Mary Beth Long, United States Assistant Secretary of State for International Security and Nonproliferation from 2007 to 2009, argued in favor of several important considerations for understanding how to better position ourselves for an effective transition in Afghanistan.

INTRODUCTION

This chapter asserts that the central challenge of the Afghan conflict is the question of how U.S. and allied forces should assist the central government in securing its international borders and policing internal populations. The purpose for the analysis is to identify what steps the DOD must take to assist Afghan security forces in professionalizing police and border patrols in preparation for a future U.S. military withdrawal.

This perspective fundamentally differs from others by setting a high priority on Afghan security while conceding low expectations for political development over the short and medium term. This analysis also assumes that elements of the Taliban insurgency will remain active after major U.S. combat operations in Afghanistan have officially concluded. Finally, it contends that American and allied development assistance will continue to flow to Afghanistan after the bulk of American military personnel have been re-deployed elsewhere.

The results of this analysis are contained in a list of recommendations in the final section of this Chapter. They demonstrate two organizing principles for the development of an effective Afghan security force: (1) the emphasis of quality over quantity, and (2) the adoption of a decentralized approach to rural justice and enforcement. These pragmatic recommendations are not intended to represent an ideal endstate for the development of Afghanistan, however, it may represent an appropriate medium-term goal for American military involvement.

CONFRONTING THE TALIBAN WITH A CT/COIN MIX

The Taliban insurgency represents the biggest threat to the creation of a stable Afghan security force. Among American military experts, the debate continues regarding the preferred model for confronting this dangerous and capable Afghan enemy; counterinsurgency (COIN), or counterterrorism (CT).[1] Though the current U.S. plan is a composite that includes elements of both strategies, it relies most heavily on COIN.

This is also known as the Petraeus-McChrystal model, and emphasizes the protection of local populations from insurgent intimidation and the importance of establishing cooperative relations among traditional community leaders.

---

[1]   Bob Woodward has captured this well in his book *Obama's Wars* (Woodward, Bob., 2010. *Obama's Wars*. New York: Simon & Schuster).

The chief disadvantage of an Afghan COIN strategy, from the U.S. perspective, is that it remains "resource intensive" by committing large numbers of allied personnel and development assistance to a decades-long conflict.[2] These unremittingly high military expenditures are politically taxing and have the effect of skewing the U.S. force structure to the "low end" in order to accommodate sustained combat operations abroad.

Further, the U.S. is not effectively organized to re-engineer societies. Thus, it is problematic that the U.S. has either the willpower and staying power or the capabilities to see such a COIN campaign through to a successful endgame.

CT, on the other hand, represents a more limited, adversary-focused strategy designed to aggressively root out enemy strong-holds rather than fortifying large numbers of friendly population centers. Vice President Biden has advocated this approach, arguing that CT's relatively low costs in terms of deployed ground forces and higher reliance on technical intelligence and advanced equipment are elements that play to American strengths. Critics maintain, however, that intermittent air strikes and Special Operations missions do not adequately demonstrate American commitment to the region. Moreover, they contend CT is not a viable strategy for undermining an insurgency and stabilizing an impoverished, war-torn country like Afghanistan.

Regardless, as we enter the 10th year of what has become the longest war in U.S. history, the stakes in Afghanistan are indisputably high. Building a capable 400,000 man force will need to directly confront national, provincial, district, and tribal divisions; corruption; and illiteracy— to name just three of the challenges. Transition to an Afghan lead and a developmental focus, however it is managed, will be elusive and not well determined by arbitrary dates, be they 2011, 2014, or ....

TRAINING THE AFGHAN NATIONAL POLICE— THE KEY TO THE CONFLICT

The fundamental challenge for the new Afghan regime will be its ability to develop an effective Afghan National Police (ANP) force. Lieutenant General William Caldwell, Commander of the U.S. and NATO training mission in Afghanistan, highlighted this in a *60 Minutes* interview broadcast on November 30, 2010.[3] Consequently, the most critical U.S. and allied

---

[2]   Its defining document is Army Field Manual 3–24.

[3]   *60 Minutes*. CBS and WCBS Television, New York, Nov. 30, 2009.

mission in Afghanistan will be helping the central government train and equip the ANP to coordinate its operations with the Afghan National Army and become a force capable of winning the respect and confidence of the Afghan people (Figure 1).

Understanding the ANP

The ANP is comprised of four components:

1. **Afghan Uniform Police (AUP):** Single largest policing element. Responsible for general law enforcement, public safety, internal security.
2. **Afghan National Civil Order Police (ANCOP):** An elite force that patrols high threat areas and is used for civil disturbances (equivalent to American SWAT teams).
3. **Afghan Border Police (ABP):** Patrol Afghanistan's border.
4. **Counter-Narcotics Police–Afghanistan (CNP–A)*:** Eliminate narcotics production and trafficking of illicit drugs.

Figure 1: Understanding the Afghan National Police (ANP).

According to Joseph Keefe,[4] the International Security Assistance Force (ISAF) and Afghanistan's Ministry of the Interior have taken the lead in developing Afghanistan's main police training program, called the *Focused District Development Concept (FDD)*. The aim of this six-phase program was initially to reform and professionalize local police units in Afghanistan's 365 districts that have relied on traditional "warlord" practices for enforcing order, such as beatings and extortion.[5]

FOCUSED DISTRICT DEVELOPMENT PROGRAM

The FDD is multi-phase program designed to remove and retrain local police for a period of eight weeks, then return and re-integrate the units to their home districts. It is constructed around a 10-month cycle.

---

[4]   Joseph D. Keefe is a Research Staff Member for the Institute of Defense Analyses. He has also worked for the Office of National Drug Control Policy, and with the U.S. DEA. Many of the views that follow represent his arguments presented at the National Defense University conference "Policing and COIN Operations," on September 29, 2010.

[5]   The FDD's primary mission has recently been expanded to include the introduction of modest judicial reforms and reconstruction projects.

Though the FDD program was initially conceived as a means of professionalizing ANP units, its primary mission has been co-opted and the program transformed into a platform for training local security forces in COIN tactics. Critically, the FDD's eight-week curriculum now offers less than a week of actual "police training." The remaining seven weeks are devoted to safety/survival instruction, terrorist tactics, counterterrorism, defense, and weapons qualification (Figure 2). This dearth of police investigative and enforcement training has left ANP units inadequately prepared to execute their primary mission at the local level and confused their role as combatants in the COIN fight. As a consequence, ill-equipped units are frequently deployed to hostile areas where they are outnumbered, with limited reinforcements and inadequate armament.[6]

Phase 1.	6 to 8 weeks	District assessment
Phase 2.	10 to 14 days	Relief in place by a covering security force (usually ANCOP)
Phase 3.	8 weeks (plus movement time)	Reconstitution of the district police force – reorganizing, retraining, re-equipping, reviewing the renovation/construction of facilities
Phase 4.	1 week	Reinsertion of the trained and reformed police force back into its district
Phase 5.	2 to 4 months	Mentoring by a Police Mentor Team (PMT) with continued collective training in the district; concludes when district police force is validated as capable of independent operations
Phase 6.	Indefinite	Operational overwatch and sustainment training by the PMT

Figure 2: The Focused District Development (FDD) Program concept.

ENDURING CHALLENGES: STRUCTURE, LITERACY, CORRUPTION, RESOURCES

Any conceivable training program for the ANP faces an impressive number of cultural, institutional, and financial obstacles. Foremost among these is

---

[6] The FDD curriculum has practically created "low-cost trigger-pullers" with high casualty rates (2007–June 2009 = 1,764 KIA/2,885 WIA), high attrition rates (15–30%/yr), and low morale.

the top-down, nationalized approach to policing counter to Afghan culture, which has historically been decentralized. The central government has generally not been present in these significant functions.

Second is the endemic lack of literacy and math skills among local recruits. According to recent estimates, the ANP suffers from a literacy rate of less than 25%, and many personnel are unable to do elementary arithmetic.[7] Such low rates of literacy pose intractable accountability, management, and training problems for a force devoted to enforcing the rule of law.

Third, but perhaps an equally intransigent difficulty, is the pervasive culture of corruption accepted at all organizational levels. The corrosive effect of institutional graft handicaps the effective training and administration of Afghanistan's judicial and security apparatus while, more broadly, undermining the population's confidence in the state itself.

A final difficulty lies in the ANP's relative poverty. New recruits are indoctrinated into the organization's culture of scarcity where low pay, inadequate equipment, and low levels prestige create "hoarding" behavior and the expectation of abandonment. A dearth of new equipment and the inability to maintain old gear ensures the ANP remains a chronically under-armed force.

ANP OPERATIONAL VULNERABILITIES

FDD training challenges generally reflect Afghanistan's broader problems with the ANP. Low rates of literacy and math, endemic corruption, and lack of official resources have resulted in an organization which is neither effective nor sustainable. Yet at an annual cost of $1B/year (estimate 2008) for pay, training, equipment, and O&M, the current ANP budget matches Afghanistan's entire annual national income. What has the central government purchased for such significant investment? In many ways, the funds have produced an ANP defined by scarcity, rather than organizational effectiveness. The analysis found significant shortages and vulnerabilities in the following areas:

Equipment.
- Immature logistics capability and transportation infrastructure.
- Culture of poverty that creates "hoarding"/expectation of abandonment.

---

[7]   A national program, called the ANSF Literacy Program.

- Inability to maintain existing equipment.
- An under-armed ANP vis-a-vis the Taliban.

Wages and Payment.
- According to 2009 data, ANP pay of $165/month (with hazard pay up to $240/month) cannot compete with Taliban fighters earning $300/month.
- The electronic payment system has many serious issues as GIRoA moves to a national banking system. Currently there are only 50 "bank outlets" in the country.

Pervasive Corruption.
- Corruption exists at all levels within the ANP, which the population views as the face of the GIRoA.
- Unsurprisingly, the population does not trust the police, whose confidence is also undermined by low and diminishing international regard.

Accountability Systems.
- Lack of *internal affairs units* at the provincial level impose severe leadership and management challenges on the system.
- Limited recognition of informal security and justice structures means that there is little or no synchronized approach to *justice reform/Rule of Law*. Police, courts, and the entire penal corrections systems is woefully lacking generally and uncoordinated throughout.[8]

Police Mentor Teams.
- In May 2009: 2,375 personnel were required, yet only 922 personnel were assigned (39%).
- As security forces grow to the expected 160,000, shortfalls will become even more acute.

---

[8] The top-down, nationalized approach to policing is counter to Afghan culture, which has historically been decentralized. The central government has generally not been present in these significant functions.

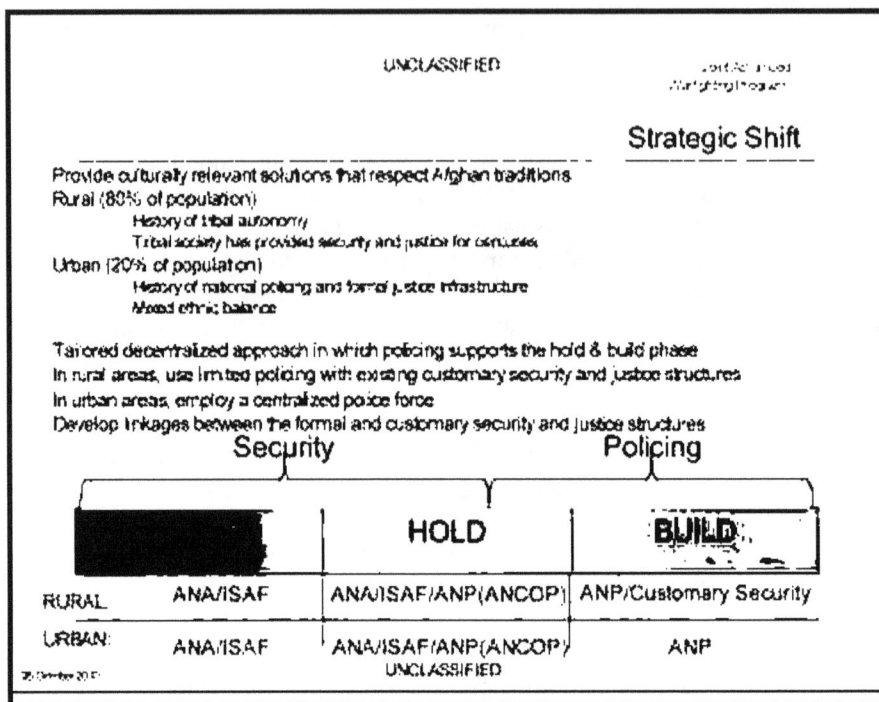

Figure 3: Strategic Shift.

In sum, the above strongly suggests that (A) the Afghan National Police
is neither a capable security force nor a capable police force; and (B) A
holistic overall of the GIRoA approach to justice reform is in order — a new
strategy that is culturally and resource relevant to the ANP's critical mission.
Some might call this a "strategic shift," as represented in Figure 3. This shift
would require prioritizing a substantial number of adjustments in thinking
about policing and structuring the ANP. These are expressed in the
following list of priorities to make the ANP more effective.

FIVE PRIORITIES FOR A MORE EFFECTIVE ANP

1. Emphasize Quality.
   • Train and equip a smaller, more capable force.[9]

---

[9] Reduction in ANP numbers could be used to increase ANA numbers.

- Use incentives (pay, specialty pay, awards, re-enlistment bonus) to induce career versus conscription environment.
- Build and sustain In-Service Training.

2. Narrow the Mission.
   - ANP should be used for policing, not as a substitute for ANA security forces.
   - Emphasize closer coordination between ANA and ANP units.

3. Revise Police Training.
   - Expand curriculum and increase training to emphasize police instruction.
   - Provide continuous mentoring and performance assessments.

4. Leverage Customary Security and Justice Structures in Rural and Urban Areas.
   - Commission on Conflict Mediation—akin to out-of-court arbitration for resource and land-based conflicts.
   - Support the shura/jirga by improving existing mechanisms.
   - Register shuras/jirgas with district government.
   - Record decisions at district level.
   - Processes to move cases between formal and customary systems.

5. Increase Literacy and Human Capital.
   - Mandatory math and literacy training programs.
   - Create (secular) educational opportunities in the workplace; advertise benefits.
   - Emphasize importance of written police reports in the collection of evidence and preparation for testimony and prosecution.

THE STRATEGIC CHALLENGE—APPLYING WHAT WE THINK WE KNOW TO UNIQUE CIRCUMSTANCES

T.X. Hammes[10] argued that a successful COIN campaign must be police-led, intelligence-driven, and population-centric. Beyond that COIN campaigns can be differentiated along five vectors or lines of operation of which the counterinsurgent controls only three of the five.

1. Domestic or expeditionary;

2. Direct or indirect support of host nation;

3. Major or minor commitment;

4. Unitary or fragmented enemy; and

5. Single sponsor or coalition.

Kalev "Gunner" Sepp's extensive review of lessons learned from 54 20th-century insurgencies and COIN responses[11] left us pessimistic for finding answers in history. Afghanistan is "unique." Key problems common in both Iraq and Afghanistan include the following:

1. Corruption rampant.

2. Abuse of population,

3. Training too short.

4. Training poorly done.

5. Too few trainers, even fewer mentors.

---

[10] T.X. Hammes is a Senior Research Fellow at the Institute for National Strategic Studies, National Defense University, and a 30-year veteran of the USMC. He is the author of over 100 articles and book chapters on military history and strategy, and of the recent groundbreaking volume, *The Sling and the Stone: On War in the 21st Century.*

[11] Dr. Kalev I. Sepp is currently a Senior Lecturer in Defense Analysis at the U.S. Naval Postgraduate School in Monterey, California. Until January 2009, he served as the Deputy Assistant Secretary of Defense for Special Operations Capabilities. Dr. Sepp earned his Ph.D. at Harvard University and served in the U.S. Army Special Forces.

6. Cultural conflicts.

7. Little or no Rule of Law—and linking security forces to rule of law and governance challenges.

THREE WAYS TO CONCEPTUALIZE INSURGENCIES/COIN

Steve Metz[12] posited that the central problem is that we tried to polish and apply 20th-century insurgency principles to 21st-century conflicts that differ in fundamental ways. Moreover, excessive focusing on operation/tactical levels contributes to the problem, if, indeed, the strategy itself is flawed.

1. As a variant of war, one way to think of insurgency/COIN is as *enemy-centric* in which the objective is victory. It is DOD-heavy with emphasis on bilateral mil-to-mil partnerships and military train-and-equip programs.

2. Insurgency is a violent competition for support; hence, the insurgency/COIN is *population-centric*. This is the essence of FM 3–24 and dependent on the insurgents needing population support, and that such support really is up for grabs. Liens of emphasis here include psyops and a transition from military to aid programs.

3. The insurgency/COIN is part of a larger social pathology. It is *system-centric* in which the lack of economic capacity is a pre-eminent challenge. These kinds of transformations will directly threaten the existing empowered elites. Further, the U.S. is not effectively organized to re-engineer societies. Thus, it is highly unlikely that it has either the willpower and staying power and the capabilities to see such a COIN campaign through to a successful endgame.

---

[12] Dr. Stephen Metz is currently the Chairman of the Regional Strategy and Planning Department at the U.S. Army War College Strategic Studies Institute. He is the author of more than 100 publications on future war and a frequent contributor to strategic and military trade journals. Dr. Metz received his Ph.D. in political science from the Johns Hopkins University.

SEVEN KEY CONSIDERATIONS FOR
WINNING AFGHANISTAN

Mary Beth Long[13] argued in favor of several important considerations for understanding how to better position ourselves for an effective transition in Afghanistan.

U.S. forces have been particularly prone to judge their military success by the number of killed and captured enemy forces on the battlefield. American commanders have often predicted the collapse of the Taliban, and yet, year after year, the strength of this dangerous adversary has remained practically undiminished. This analysis has yielded a number of key insights which, taken together, help to explain the Taliban's impressive regenerative ability and the way forward for U.S. and coalition strategy in the region:

1. Long-term Commitment: The Afghans want predictability—and reliability, which they do not see from the American commitment—and a proposed withdrawal date of July 2011. This is why one of the reasons the Taliban succeeds the way it does. It is there for the long haul—and will be a force to deal with long after U.S. Forces return home. Long-term COIN operations are needed—a generational commitment.

2. Lower Political Expectations: The Afghans look forward to a modest future. U.S. and allied forces should also lower expectations for achieving a perfect representative government in Afghanistan. An achievable exit strategy for American forces is to leave behind a relatively stable Afghanistan capable of defending its internal and external territory, and organized to effectively absorb development assistance over the medium and long term.

3. Leave the Wire Behind: Embassy and coalition forces based in Afghanistan remain too often behind the protective cultural and military umbrella of an armed compound. This chronic lack of engagement with the Afghans prevents American forces from understanding the priorities of local populations and forming mutually productive alliances with members of the community.

[13]   Ms. Mary Beth Long was United States Assistant Secretary of State for International Security and Nonproliferation from 2007 to 2009. She worked for over 13 years at the Central Intelligence Agency's Directorate of Operations on a variety of international issues, and has earned several awards for her distinguished service.

4. Focus on the Youth: American and Allied commanders should begin treating Afghan youth as a key constituency. The median age in Afghanistan is less than 20 years old. Those 16 to 21-year-old youths of today were 7 to 12 years old on September 11, 2001. Many villages have median ages approaching 17. These young adults do not remember the Soviet invasion, and their world views are fundamentally different from older generations. Young Afghans are more tolerant of Western views than older (40 to 50-year-old) generations.[14] Afghan adults have less influence on their family than we suppose, yet they take up the bulk of American attentions in our relations with local communities.

5. Advertise, Inform, and Engage: U.S. information and psychological operations campaigns have been largely ineffective and should be re-evaluated. Reaching out to the public is as important for the stability of the country as training and equipping security forces.

6. Local Commanders: A major weakness of the American and coalition system has been the relatively rapid rotation cycles of local commanders. This means relations with community leaders are routinely destroyed as military and contractor personnel leave for other assignments or are sent home. Twelve month tours do not equal the kind of individual-based staying power that can develop the kinds of personal relationships so necessary in this familial and tribal-based society. Equally important, when in country, we cannot live and operate behind the wired compounds.

7. Re-evaluate Alliances: The DoD should re-evaluate the effectiveness of two American allies in the Afghan conflict; NATO security forces and private contractors. Often 40–60% of a team in-country are contractors. NATO is not currently prepared for COIN doctrinal analysis, which means the U.S. often must drag them through the process. Perhaps new alliances and partners are required.

---

[14] When we started worrying about the Taliban, most of the Afghan population was under 10 years old. They think the golden years were 2004–2006 when they attended school. Then, all of a sudden, U.S. soldiers entered their country.

CONCLUSION

Wicked problems may indeed be the best characterization of policing and COIN operations in Afghanistan. Surely, we face problems that are difficult to solve because of incomplete, changing, and/or contradictory requirements. Further, just when we believe we have addressed an issue, new problems jump to the forefront.

Perhaps the Obama administration has moved in the right direction when it shared publicly a reined set of expectations for "success" in Afghanistan. Regardless, the U.S. and the NATO community are not likely to execute a precipitous and complete withdrawal from Afghanistan in 2011 or 2014. The engagement will evolve and change in style and substance, but engaged we will be. The challenge to all of us remains: to apply what we know to unique circumstances; be flexible and capable of adjusting as warranted; and be sensitive to the realities of the host nation in which we are operating.

Chapter 8: Building Indigenous Capacity[1]

Samuel Musa

Senior Research Fellow
Center for Technology and National Security Policy
National Defense University, Fort McNair

John Morgan

Deputy Director for Science and Technology
Counter-Terrorism Technical Support Office (CTTSO)
United States Department of Defense

Matt Keegan

Visiting Fellow, Center for Technology and National Security Policy
National Defense University, Fort McNair
and Chief of Staff and Vice President, U.S. Strategy
Selex Galileo, Inc., Arlington, Virginia

The panel members for the Roundtable: Building Indigenous Capacity were Mr. Frank Prendergast, Dr. James Bruce, and Mr. Judd Ray. Mr. Frank Prendergast is a member of the Australian Federal Police, an expeditionary tool of Australian foreign policy. The AFP supports stability response, security intervention, and long-term community policing and is a formation unlike anything in the USG national security community. Dr. James Bruce, Senior Political Scientist of the RAND Corporation, spent his career in the CIA working both for the Directorate of Operations and Directorate of Intelligence Analysis. Dr. Bruce's most recent work for the RAND Corporation concerns his evaluation of "Project LEGACY," the largest effort by the U.S. Government since Vietnam to develop an indigenous police information gathering and analysis capability for COIN. This Chapter attempts to document these two expert perspectives. Mr. Judd Ray is a member of ICITAP, and is currently assigned as the program manager for the Active component of the Civilian Response Corps (CRC–A). Mr. Ray's career in law enforcement spans over 38 years—including 25 years with the Federal Bureau of Investigation (FBI).

---

[1]   The authors acknowledge the contributions of Drew Lomax. His input formed the foundation of the chapter.

INTRODUCTION

The early stages of the War on Terror spawned hope and even hubris among Defense planners. Small numbers of American troops wielding unrivaled lethal technology seemed to topple or "decapitate" regimes at will. Early images of Special Forces soldiers and CIA paramilitary operators on horseback with Northern Alliance guerrillas in Afghanistan were seen by some to signal the completion of a revolution in military affairs. But by the autumn of 2003, an accelerating insurgency in Iraq signaled that these wars were veering off script.

By 2005, inside-the-beltway wisdom conceded that the promises of high-tech, "full spectrum dominance" were not sufficient to manage the situation, particularly in Iraq. Concurrent with other on-the-fly changes to operations on the ground, DoD issued Directive 3000.05, and soon published a much-lauded COIN Doctrine, authored by General David Petraeus.

DoD Instruction 3000.05, "Military Support for Stability, Security, Transition, and Reconstruction (SSTR) Operations," emphasized the development of police and governance structures during stability operations, elevating these so-called "soft" skill sets to a level of parity with major high-intensity combat operations. General Petraeus's designation of 2006 as the "year of the police," during some of the most difficult days of the Iraq war, heralded a new manpower-intensive phase of the post-9/11 campaigns: "shock and awe" and "full spectrum dominance" were now little more than discredited marketing slogans.

More than four years later, and nearly a decade after the invasion into Afghanistan, more than 200,000 American Servicemembers—along with untold numbers of civil servants, other government agencies, NGOs, and contractors—continue to try to secure peace and stability in these troubled regions.

Today it is conventional wisdom among COIN planners that the development of indigenous capacity—whether in the "host-nation's" Army, police or other security services—is the main effort in COIN campaigns. Yet the manner in which the United States Government (USG) builds indigenous security services' capacity remains ad hoc and is essentially a task, when performed at any Iraq- or Afghanistan-scale, carried out by a conglomeration of U.S. Military and a private army of contractors.

Despite such formal recognition that police are instrumental to COIN, and after a decade of recent lessons learned in the current South Asian wars, there remains room to investigate further the intersection of policing and COIN. To this end, the National Defense University and the Combating Terrorism Technical Support Office convened a workshop with experts comprising law enforcement and the military, COIN practitioners, and academics. The panel activities during *Roundtable VI: Building Indigenous Capacity* discussed how to build indigenous capacity among host nation forces during COIN operations.

MR. FRANK PRENDERGAST: THE AUSTRALIAN FEDERAL POLICE— INTERNATIONAL DEPLOYMENT GROUP

Mr. Prendergast opened the discussion with an overview of the Australian Federal Police's (AFP) International Deployment Group (IDG), its roles, mission, and organization. Formed in 2004, IDG is comprised of 1,000 personnel and maintains the readiness to deploy abroad at any given time. Mr. Prendergast was careful to stress that the AFP's IDG is neither a gendarmerie nor a paramilitary force. The IDG is concerned with stability response and long-term community policing, capacity-building, and is a tool of Australian foreign policy.

In addition to developing policy and the design and evaluation of police-force interventions into trouble areas, the IDG conducts a wide range of operational activities. These include training, both in the academic/classroom setting and in tactical/field environs. "We don't train people to be police officers. We train them to train others," Mr. Prendertast reiterated.

Mr. Prendergast then explained the rationale for maintaining such a force. The Australian government invests $300 million annually in the IDG, a testament to Canberra's recognition that police capacity can play a vital, preventive role abroad and may in this fashion provide an alternative to military intervention.

Investment in the IDG reflects an understanding of the importance of the rule of law—strong association with the rule of law and development outcomes. International indicators point to the key importance of the rule of law in international development—there is "not much bang for your buck from aid assistance without rule of law," noted Mr. Prendergast. "We have recognized that there has to be a capacity development of the indigenous police force. If that does not happen, what is the exit strategy then? Much of our focus is on capacity-building," said Prendergast.

The confidence of the local community is an indicator of the effectiveness of any police force. To this end, the IDG focuses its efforts on institutional strengthening. In so far as COIN is a consideration, Mr. Prendergast offered that without a sustained attention to the indigenous capacity, there can be no success in the mission. He also stressed the correlation between increases in stability and larger role for police, i.e., police responsibilities increase with stability and decline of violence.

Using the now familiar "clear, hold, build" as a framework, the military or other security organizations clear and reduce the most capable threats, and the police provide the enduring, local security knowledge and first line of defense in security stability. The Australian Federal Police are developing joint-training, joint-exercise and exchanges with Australian Defense Forces (ADF). Mr. Prendergast also described the Australian interagency/joint task force structure, where command may reside with either the police or the military. In some contingencies, AFP operates under ADF control, and in many environments ADF operates under the AFP. This type of work has been representative of AFP IDG operations the last few years and reflects a clear understanding of roles and missions: "We subscribe to the assertion that the military and police have different roles, and we clearly delineate differences between roles of military and police."

While Mr. Prendergast noted that the AFP is currently active and working effectively in Afghanistan, it was in other regions where he felt their impact was best illustrated and where the characteristics of the force described earlier could be observed. During the Regional Assistance Mission–Solomon Islands beginning in 2003, the AFP's IDG participated in a 6-nation law and order intervention, backed up by a small military force. It was stressed that this was not a military intervention and that the principal aim of the deployment, insofar as the IDG was concerned, was to bring under control the indigenous police force.

It is important to account for the scale of this intervention into a nation of roughly 600,000 people in a maritime environment. The original force set up by the British had disintegrated and the main task for the IDG upon arrival was to restore law and order and to begin to implement programs to start to deal with endemic corruption. "While we were working through the security process, we were looking down the road to what happens once the intervention force departs," he noted.

Security in the Solomon intervention has waxed and waned depending on the circumstances on the ground. The IDG's activities have moved towards capacity development supporting regional elections in 2006. Since

2006, IDG has been engaged in continuous capacity development through the most recent general elections in August 2010. These efforts included institutional strengthening, as police mentoring is only one dimension of stabilization operations. IDG oversaw the implementation of literacy, housing and health programs and "in the process we are identifying future leaders," said Prendergast.

In closing, Mr. Prendergast stressed the importance of identifying what is culturally appropriate in a given situation. He offered that police training/mentoring has real limitations: dialogue must continue on these ongoing issues; institutional strengthening is as important as actual police training.

DR. JAMES BRUCE: EVALUATING LEGACY

The panel turned next to a presentation by Dr. Bruce on the LEGACY program. LEGACY is the largest effort by the U.S. Government since the Vietnam War to develop an indigenous police information gathering and analysis capability for COIN. Dr. Bruce's presentation offered highlights, and it identified lessons-learned during implementation of the program in Iraq, which is now ongoing in Afghanistan. It should be noted that LEGACY builds specialized capacity for local police forces; it is not primarily about law enforcement or even the rule of law. Rather, LEGACY seeks to build from a zero-baseline in twenty months a functioning host-nation intelligence bureaucracy that can penetrate and defeat localized insurgent actors.

Dr. Bruce described two specific implementations of the program in Iraq—LEGACY, first as a pilot initiative in Al Anbar, supported by the USMC; and GRYPHON, which was an expansion of LEGACY into four more provinces (Ninevah, Salah ad Din, Kirkuk, and Diyala—in Multi-national Division–North (MND–N)).

The doctrine from which LEGACY mentors instruct is derived from the British experience in COIN, specifically the intelligence model that developed within the U.K. "Special Branch" and which was used to great effect during the Troubles in Northern Ireland. Dr. Bruce stressed the uniqueness of the Special Branch approach, which has no counterpart in U.S. experience. This is a serious and significant differentiation from the standard resource pool of mentoring/training, which the U.S. typically contracts from among U.S. police forces that have no historic experience in COIN or in police intelligence operations. Additionally, U.S. laws prohibit the transmission of U.S. tradecraft to foreign organizations or individuals, thus the U.K. intelligence model developed under LEGACY is ideally suited to building indigenous intelligence capacity.

Effective COIN operations are inherently intelligence-driven. Improved targeting ensures that counterinsurgent forces do not kill or capture the wrong people and thereby worsen local grievances and erode public support for the government. LEGACY sought to, and achieved, improved generation of meaningful intelligence by host-nation security forces in Al Anbar and in MND–North.

In Al Anbar, contractor teams comprised of former U.K. Special Branch police mentors and Accredited Cultural Advisors (security-cleared linguists) were emplaced in January 2008 where they mentored, trained, and advised Iraqi and U.S. Forces through September 2009. These teams were embedded within U.S. military Police Transition Teams (PTTs), who partnered with local Iraqi police in order to build local security capacity. The role of the ACA was particularly crucial as the mentoring of local Iraqi police and military required a credible, culturally attuned interlocutor between the Special Branch mentor and the host-nation (Iraqi) security personnel.

The RAND Corporation evaluated how well the LEGACY program worked. The evaluation methodology considered infrastructure, performance, effectiveness, and impact. Aside from the obvious infrastructure status, which can quickly be evaluated and monitored for improvement, metrics for such skill sets are hard to consider, but basically amount to "Are they doing it how they are supposed to be doing it? And is there an operational impact?" Dr. Bruce reported that the reporting on both the Anbar (LEGACY) and MND–North (GRYPHON) implementation of the program was promising and showed that the program was largely effective.

In Anbar province, mentor teams enjoyed near continual proximity to the Iraqis as the mentor teams were embedded within the PTTs. But in Gryphon program mentors were not embedded and in most cases had to "commute" from bases along with the PTTs to which they were attached. This posture was the result of more restrictive policies that originated in the then-new Status of Forces Agreement between U.S. Forces and Iraq. This distinction highlights one of the principal lessons learned: embedding the mentors is a highly effective means of employment, but the "commuter" model, not surprisingly, did not work as well.

Overall, RAND concluded that the LEGACY program was effective in Iraq. While police professionalization involves implementing the provisions of the rule of law, the development of an effective intelligence capability is another critical attribute of a host-nation security force that must stand on its own after U.S. withdrawal during an active and deep-rooted insurgency. LEGACY equipped the Iraqi organizations that they mentored with the capability to develop local knowledge and intelligence of value for the counterinsurgency.

LESSONS IDENTIFIED

RAND identified 10 lessons learned throughout their evaluation of the LEGACY program, which have been integrated into the LEGACY program's operations in Afghanistan and which might be of value to other similar mentor-advising capacity development efforts. Chief among these was that on-site, continuous embedded posture is most effective; in other words, "handholding" is more effective than remote monitoring.

Additionally, for a program like LEGACY to succeed, the U.S. military must recognize police training is an integral part of COIN. In Al Anbar and in MND–N the U.S. Marine Corps and the U.S. Army, respectively, largely did so. Dr. Bruce noted that this does not come easy for the military, but nevertheless the operational customers of LEGACY and GRYPHON (i.e., the local U.S. Military units) did view police support and integration are crucial.

The host nation must also support and embrace a capacity-building program; there has to be buy-in from the national to the province and district level. In the Anbar province, support was needed, but it could not be acquired from Baghdad. So the LEGACY program emplaced a liaison officer at the Ministry of Interior, a predominantly Shia Ministry, to track and pressure for resources. But steady, reliable support for the predominantly Sunni province of Al Anbar remained an ongoing and uneven concern. In a similar way, in such a capacity-building program as LEGACY, where the principal actors are contractors (and in the case of LEGACY, U.K. and thus foreign), buy-in from the U.S. military for security/force protection, communication, etc. is absolutely essential.

Cultural sensitivity was also important. The LEGACY program benefited greatly from culturally-attuned advisors (ACAs) at every level. Understanding the local and national culture was crucial; where such understanding was better, the results were better as well.

A final characteristic of the LEGACY program which distinguished it from other U.S. resourced capacity-building efforts was the presence of a comprehensive and proven doctrine that is continually updated as new lessons are learned. LEGACY benefited from more than 1,200 pages of USG-approved tactics, techniques, and procedures which professionalized not only the host-nation charges who were mentored, but also provided a consistent script for the mentors and ACAs, ensuring a professional delivery.

There must also be a mechanism to demonstrate that learning from the instruction and doctrine is occurring and to ensure mentor/staff compliance. LEGACY employs a cadre of Compliance Officers who act like program auditors and who visit the mentoring locations monthly to evaluate the progress and to prescribe corrective action in concert with the locally supported U.S. military command.

MR. JUDSON RAY: POLICY CONSIDERATIONS

Mr. Ray's approach was to ask questions. In particular, he asked:

- "What is the transportability of the Western experience to the ungoverned areas of the world?" I cannot answer this question.

- "If the police could achieve their goals with their methods, would we as Westerners be satisfied?" My experience is "no." Our overarching USG goals are often not the same as what the indigenous police are willing to accept. I bring this to ask the final question:

- "Why are we doing this?" "It's kind of ironic, because as a matter of policy, [in] the Foreign Assistance Act, it says that we don't do this. If there are precedents saying we don't do this, how are we going to do this now?"

He stated that we need to re-look at this from the point of view of policy. He said that "I look at all this for one reason only, as a police officer—will these capacity-building policies improve our national security? How will police training improve our national security?" In his experience, the investigative mandate of the USG agencies stops at the water's edge. We are totally dependent on the capacity of the local police ability to protect our citizens and interests—"if you are not looking at the mission of the FBI, we don't need you." Why can't we develop something similar to what the Australians have?"

He was sent to Saudi Arabia right after September 11, 2001. His experience in the region led him to ask more questions: "What laws are we concerned with? And whose laws? Where do we begin?" There is a failure to look at this holistically; you cannot stovepipe this operation. "At what point does an environment become permissive enough to put a Western police perspective in the field?" I can't find anyone to tell me that. What we have to do is to climb Mount Everest, but we don't even have the team at base camp. We have to test, operate, re-test, and exit.

SOME QUESTIONS

The panel concluded with questions of Mr. Prendergast, Dr. Bruce, and Mr. Ray in regards to what they had presented. Mr. Prendergast described the development of metrics in capacity-building, noting that they generally remained an ongoing concern in any operation and developed throughout the engagement. Dr. Bruce spoke to a question regarding resources and exit strategy. And Mr. Prendergast followed up with a description of how the IDG is organized and manned, noting that enjoys human resources from among Australian state police through a reimbursement framework with the states. Mr. Ray mentioned that he would consider ICITAP at base camp. However, he indicated that most of the funding comes from INL for the DOJ programs around the world. DOJ funds only six positions at ICITAP and any expansion has yet to happen. Until they have their own budget, it will be more of the same.

CLOSING THOUGHTS

American COIN doctrine is filled with references to "host nations," governments ostensibly and willingly harboring/hosting a foreign counterinsurgent force or source of assistance. It was beyond the scope of this paper and indeed the NDU-sponsored conference to fully explore the various modalities of COIN—e.g., COIN, where the principal counterinsurgent force is foreign; those COIN campaigns where the counterinsurgent is the threatened regime/government itself and stands alone. But what was discussed in the one-day event must be considered in the context of relatively historical reflection.

An invading or foreign power hoping to re-order a state is inherently deeply disadvantaged, particularly to the extent to which it relies upon the invading/intervening power's own (and inherently foreign) structure as the basis for the new state's re-ordering. As Van Crevald notes, and which Ho Chi Minh and Mao demonstrated, time is the key factor in counterinsurgency.

At a time of declining public support for large-scale, monumentally expensive entanglements abroad, the U.S.-led campaigns in Afghanistan and Iraq may be outliers and paradoxically just might belie those very doctrinal artifacts—FM 3–24 and DODI 3000.5—which elevate "stability operations" to parity with major combat operations. After trillions of dollars spent on Iraq and Afghanistan, the preventive model of intervention at limited scale evident in the AFP's IDG may be a more sustainable approach going forward.

Finally, it must be noted that the vast majority of the technical/tactical activities—the very DODI 3000.05 "soft skill sets"—carried out under the banner of "capacity-building" are performed by private contractors. There are doubtlessly advantages and strong arguments in favor of this arrangement. Americans may not be enamored with so-called mercenaries or their modern-day cousins, the contingency contractors who are working for the USG in Iraq and Afghanistan by the hundreds of thousands. But they dislike the notion of sending their loved ones to godforsaken corners of the globe even more.

Perhaps the notion of converting so much of our nation's military effort and attendant sacrifice to a for-profit motive in lieu of patriotic duty says profound things about the relationship between the American people and their government. "Indeed," writes historian Andrew Bacevich, "the privatization of war—evident in the prominence achieved by armies-for-rent such as the notorious Blackwater—suggests a tacit willingness to transform military service from a civic function into an economic enterprise, with money rather than patriotism the motive."[2]

---

[2]   Andrew J. Bacevich, 2008. *The Limits of Power: The End of American Exceptionalism,* 1 ed. p. 155. New York: Metropolitan Books.

Chapter 9: Conclusions[1]

Samuel Musa

Senior Research Fellow
Center for Technology and National Security Policy
National Defense University, Fort McNair

John Morgan

Deputy Director for Science and Technology
Counter-Terrorism Technical Support Office (CTTSO)
United States Department of Defense

Matt Keegan

Visiting Fellow, Center for Technology and National Security Policy
National Defense University, Fort McNair,
and Chief of Staff and Vice President, U.S. Strategy,
Selex Galileo, Inc., Arlington, Virginia

There was general agreement within the workshop that police are important in counterinsurgency operations and the United States is challenged in the situations of training indigenous police and developing indigenous judicial systems. We lack national institutions that are present in other countries. For example, the Department of Defense supports a great deal of police training in Iraq and Afghanistan, while the Department of State has the responsibility for supporting police training more broadly. In both cases, the training is designed, delivered, and evaluated by contractors, a model that does not always work very well. In Afghanistan, we are working through contractors and are engaged in a multinational effort with the European Union, NATO, and perhaps 40 other countries. The level of confusion is very high. Many observers feel that no one is in charge and police development has lacked resources and strategic direction.

---

[1]   The authors acknowledge the contributions of Robert Perito to this Chapter. His summary at the workshop formed the foundation for the conclusions outlined here.

LESSONS LEARNED ABOUT POLICING AND
COIN OPERATIONS
FROM IRAQ AND AFGHANISTAN

There are many lessons learned from the Iraq and Afghanistan operations. First, there are fundamental differences in overall COIN strategies between Iraq and Afghanistan. In Iraq, the goal was and is to generate a democratic society; while in Afghanistan, the strategy continues to change. These changes in strategies made it difficult to prosecute a war with a moving endgame. Next, building the capacity for the military to move within the population was critical. This freedom of action is important to engaging the population in defeating the insurgency. As General Petraeus said, "We have learned that the only way to secure the population is to live with it." Further, there was no doctrine and the chain of command was not unified. There were a number of chains of command working in parallel and this made it difficult to identify the person in charge. Next, using a civil affairs team to partner with the police is critical to the operations. This partnership—at times combined with mentoring—resulted in a number of successful operations. In addition, attempts to impose the U.S. and Allied procedures and processes have often resulted in failure. Solutions must fit indigenous needs and capabilities. It is important to recognize that it is the Afghans' lives, their country, and their future. Ultimately, problems must have Afghan solutions. Finally, there are connections between drug traffickers, terrorists, and insurgents. Insurgents in Afghanistan are receiving money by protecting and facilitating drug trafficking across the border. In many cases, police will play a central role in responding to this challenge.

There is lack of knowledge of what the United States is trying to accomplish in Iraq and Afghanistan with respect to development of police capacity. In the 1960s, Afghanistan did have a national police force, but that history is now all but forgotten. For the present conflict, there are two alternative approaches:

1. Using police who are inferior to the U.S. as a force multiplier. We run personnel through a short train-and-equip program, give them a badge, and send them out on the streets with little attention paid to the institutions that control the police.

2. Develop the police as a force that deals with crime, builds relationships with their community, and protects the people.

Currently, most police capacity-building in Afghanistan (and elsewhere) has used the first approach. The focus has been on the use of police to enable military operations. The latter approach will pay greater dividends by connecting policing—and by extension the government—to the people being served. Afghans actually want the police to deal with criminals. To do this, police must be available, responsive, and fair. In particular, three main principles must be followed:

- The great effectiveness multiplier in the use of state power against violence is the allegiance and support of the public.

- In order for governments to gain public support, responsibility for security should be entrusted, in so far as possible, to police deployed among the population, who minimize the use of force and who act in accordance with accepted standards of human rights.

- Capturing, killing, or imprisoning people committing violent acts are unlikely to be effective as a long-term solution to insecurity unless guided by precise intelligence identifying perpetrators or infrastructure.

There are lessons that advocates of either approach can appreciate. First, COIN success should be measured by the degree to which security responsibilities have been transferred to the police. It should be measured in terms of populace served and legitimacy, not by the overall number of police trained and deployed. During the early stages of counterinsurgency, military units will be needed to maintain security in an area as long as police are unable to do this job on their own. Police assets should only be deployed when they can operate safely and be equipped to protect themselves. Once police have been established in an area, the COIN military commander can use the police as a critical intelligence tool to refine targeting of insurgents. Successful COIN depends on the judgment of local commanders about the proper mix of military and police assets at a particular moment in time. Civilian ("interagency") engagement is necessary to build indigenous police capacity. The military lacks the tools and doctrine to train, equip, and monitor police, so it is necessary to deploy civilian assets to perform this mission, especially in areas with communal violence.

OTHER APPROACHES FOR POLICE
CAPACITY DEVELOPMENT
EMERGED FROM THE WORKSHOP

Other ideas emerged from the workshop but are not necessarily aligned with either of the two main approaches to development of police capacity. First, the development of core policing and specialized police units is not necessarily mutually exclusive. Specialized police units have been very successful in many conflicts, including in Afghanistan. For example, the Drug Enforcement Administration has developed specialized anti-drug police units that have interrupted the opium trade and intercepted financial flows to insurgent groups.

We may conclude that specialized police unit development should be a priority for COIN, as long as their training reflects rule of law and other core policing doctrines. To be clear, Bayley and Perito do not share this view, because they feel the building of such special units interferes with the development of core policing capacity and undermines legitimacy.

Furthermore, police development must precede reconciliation among communal factions or with insurgent groups. It may be necessary to leverage local or tribal assets that have ambiguous loyalties or history to establish security in some areas. This could include the development of police under local ethnic control that may, for example, have Taliban leanings but that will conform to basic concepts in the rule of law. This could also mean the use of informants and police tactical teams to weaken insurgents. These choices must be made consciously and with appropriate training of those involved to minimize the possibility of abuses. When police protect citizens and bond with the community, the community then volunteers key information on where insurgents are.

Success relies on the engagement of experienced police trainers and an overall strategy with realistic expectations and ongoing performance measures. In many cases, the term "police" has been used very broadly and in not a very consistent way. We have to think through what we do and what kind of police we train—are the people at the conclusion of our training a real police force? By this, we mean: will they provide sustainable security to serve their communities?

How can we create a capacity in the U.S. Government to build such indigenous police in conflict environments? We don't have a national police force, but we do have Federal-level police officers that can be designated to take on this role (at the U.S. Marshal's Service, for example). The American policing experience in unique in the world, with 18,000 separate police forces and no single Federal oversight agency. The Federal Bureau of Investigation comes closest to this role, but it is not a traditional, community-based police agency. The Attorney General is often called the nation's top law enforcement official, but this title is based as much on the Department of Justice's (DoJ) role in Federal prosecution as any other role.

The International Criminal Investigative Training Assistance Program (ICITAP) is an office in the DoJ, not a full bureau, and falls under the jurisdiction of both the Departments of State and Justice. It lacks resources and capability to sustain police training through the use of an in-house force, such as the International Deployment Group under the Australian Federal Police.

It is in the interest of U.S. national security for the government to build a continuing capability to support police and judicial training. We might save a great deal of money by avoiding the need for military intervention while saving many lives in developing countries that lack the ability to protect their own citizens. This does not imply that we would apply Western standards of policing to every single country, but rather that we would enable police who are available, responsive, and fair to the people they serve. If we merely take a look at the cost of adventures in COIN, we would get more bang for the buck if police capacity-building and stability operations were integrated with the pre-mission planning than if those priorities followed the military and "cleaned up the mess" afterward.

THE RULE OF LAW IS A KEYSTONE OF STABILITY

In looking back at recent operations and offering lessons learned so we don't repeat the mistakes of history or have to re-learn old lessons, it is essential that the Rule of Law is a keystone of stability. Rule of Law must stem from acceptable, traditional and historic socio-cultural norms of the local region and not non-local practices from foreign sources. Successful campaigns must be whole-of-government interagency efforts in order to succeed. It requires working, training and mentoring the local populations to better their standard of living as opposed to a foreign system being levied by a perceived occupation force.

Security in the form of military forces may have a role in either kinetic operations, training, and/or Civil Military Operations (CMOs), but certainly police forces have an essential role in local, acceptable sustainment of security through local Rule of Law. Value of Civil Military Operations should not be underestimated. Within COIN Operations, CMOs have proven to be a positive method of lowering public barriers and enhancing acceptance of Government leadership. Whether military, CMOs, or police operations, the operating force must understand the socio-cultural norms of the region or risk alienating the populous and creating fertile fields for ongoing or future insurgency. Finally, as "all insurgency is local," it is the locals who must "buy in" and actively participate in establishing stability in their nation.

In OIF and OEF–A, DoD has opted for a Police-imbedded Training Team (PiTT) construct coupled with rapid indigenous police indoctrination and training capabilities to assist in capacity development for an element of establishing the Rule of Law. The other components of the Rule of Law (detainee operations and courts) lagged far behind this rudimentary development of patrolmen. A common perception is that American military and irregular warfare actions should leverage methods developed in policing to interdict insurgent or terrorist activity and enhance legitimacy of friendly governments through extension of the rule of law. In Stability Operations the Department of State and the U.S. Agency for International Development (USAID) are the lead U.S. agencies to support a host-nation's effort to establish or improve key aspects of governance to include rule of law and a variety of services.

One of the most critical aspects that is probably not understood to the integration of the role of "Rule of Law" in the past two engagements has been the timing and sequencing of when, where, and who supports development and sustainment activities of police, courts, and prisons in a fluid "seize, clear, build" COIN fight. These engagements, and development activities, are never uniform across a conflict zone.

Biographies

MR. ARIF ALIKHAN

Mr. Arif Alikhan is the Assistant Secretary for Policy Development at the Department for Homeland Security. He joined DHS from Los Angeles Mayor Antonio R. Villaraigosa's office, where he served as Deputy Mayor for Homeland Security and Public Safety. As a key adviser to the Mayor, he has led the City's efforts to develop homeland security, emergency management and law enforcement initiatives, including operational oversight of Los Angeles Police, Fire and Emergency Management departments. Before serving as Deputy Mayor, Alikhan was a career prosecutor with the U.S. Department of Justice from 1997–2006. During that time, he served as Chief of the Cyber and Intellectual Crimes Section for the U.S. Attorney's Office in Los Angeles and as a Senior Advisor to the U.S. Attorney General in Washington, D.C., where he oversaw the national Computer Hacking and Intellectual Property Program for the Department of Justice. Alikhan holds a J.D. from Loyola Law School and a B.A. from the University of California, Irvine.

MR. BRIAN BERREY

Brian Berrey is a senior advisor for the Combating Terrorism Technical Support Office's Irregular Warfare Support Program, which develops new solutions for the conduct of Irregular Warfare. Mr. Berrey manages a number of projects that leverage law enforcement lessons and methodologies to improve U.S. Forces' capabilities in today's overseas contingency operations.

DR. JAMES KEAGLE

Dr. James M. Keagle is the Director of the Transforming National Security seminar series at the Center for Technology and National Security Policy at the National Defense University. Prior to this position, Dr. Keagle was the National Defense University's Provost (effective 2004) and Vice President for Academic Affairs. Prior to these positions, he served as a professor of National Security Strategy at NDU. In that role Dr. Keagle worked as a research faculty member assisting with NDU's modeling and simulation and work with interagency education and training. Accepting an appointment to the U.S. Air Force Academy, he graduated second academically in his class in June 1974. Following graduation, he went to the University of Pittsburgh to complete his Masters of Arts degree in political science and earned a graduate certificate in Latin American studies. After a tour as a munitions maintenance officer, Dr. Keagle went on to become an assistant professor of political science at the U.S. Air Force Academy. In 1980, he went on to Princeton University where he completed both a Masters of Arts degree and Ph.D. in politics. He proudly notes his honorary Ph.D. from the Military Technical Academy of Romania—the only United States citizen so honored. Following his extensive education, Dr. Keagle's next six tours were political-military assignments that included direct access and interaction with Cabinet-level government officials on national security related matters. These assignments included work for two Combatant Commanders as a senior strategist; for the Office of Secretary of Defense pertaining to Cuba; Deputy Director, Office of the Secretary of Defense Bosnian Task Force; and for the Deputy Under Secretary of the Air Force in International Affairs as Senior Strategist. Military medals include the Defense Superior Service Award, the Legion of Merit, and the Purple Heart. Since leaving military service, Dr. Keagle has held the position of adjunct professor at a number of institutions to include: Syracuse University, American University, Central Michigan University, Catholic University, University of Colorado, and Lake Superior State College. He also holds honorary professorships with Transilvania University in Brasov, Romania, as well as the Mongolian Defense University—again, the only American so honored.

MR. MATT KEEGAN

Matt Keegan is Selex Galileo, Inc.'s (Selex) Chief of Staff, which is a role he was promoted to in 2007. In this role he is responsible for supporting the CEO in making decisions and project completion. These projects relate to strategic planning, staffing, business operations, contracts, business development, and alliances. He makes sure that all other staff members and employees carry out any new mandates, and is responsible for calling meetings in relation to personnel issues, company process, or projects. These meetings also give him an opportunity to lay out analytical and tactical strategies. Mr. Keegan came to Selex in July of 2006 as a direct hire of the CEO of Selex S&AS Ltd., to establish the position of the Vice President of Strategy (U.S.), a role he continues to play today. His primary strategic mission has continued to be to move the U.S. division of Selex out of a pure business development/product representation organization to a fully operational business. Mr. Keegan helped stand up new units such as the air integration unit, the Security Assistance unit, and the Huntsville unit, and initiated the planning and execution of the Stennis expansion plan and connective to SOCOM efforts. In his various roles, he has led major capture efforts, business development organizations, and service organizations for products, implementation services, and hosting. In all four organizations he served as a strategic advisor or in the case of his work with consultancy helped develop strategies for divisions of companies such as Northrop Grumman, McDonnell Douglas, General Dynamics, and FMC (now ATK). Mr. Keegan is a distinguished graduate of the National Defense University's Industrial College of the Armed Forces. After graduating (in the top 1%) with his M.S. (in National Resource Strategy) from NDU/ICAF, he remained a Visiting Fellow to NDU's Center for Technology and National Security Policy (CTNSP), advising on information technology solutions with a focus on the use of biometric infrastructure solutions for application in counterinsurgency warfare. Mr. Keegan has a B.A. in Political Science from Syracuse University's Maxwell School. He has written articles, case studies and white papers on a range of national security topics ranging from technology application for counterinsurgency, Pentagon procurement issues, defense market direction, and strategic planning in the post–Cold War world.

MR. DREW LOMAX

Drew Lomax is a senior program analyst for the Combating Terrorism Technical Support Office's Irregular Warfare Support Program, which develops new solutions for the conduct of Irregular Warfare. Drew manages a number of projects that leverage law enforcement lessons and methodologies to improve U.S. Forces' capabilities in today's overseas contingency operations.

DR. JOHN MORGAN

Dr. John S. Morgan serves as the Deputy Director for Science and Technology at the Counter-Terrorism Technical Support Office (CTTSO) of the Department of Defense. At CTTSO, Dr. Morgan provides scientific advice to advance the work of the Technical Support Working Group and other activities to support the combating terrorism community. He is on assignment from the Department of Justice, where he directs the Office of Science and Technology, which is responsible for development of new technology for use in law enforcement. While at the Department of Justice, Dr. Morgan received the Service to America medal for his work to advance the nation's capacity to use DNA evidence. Prior to coming to the Department of Justice, Dr. Morgan conducted research in detection and mitigation of weapons of mass destruction at the Johns Hopkins University Applied Physics Laboratory (APL). His research work at APL also included non-destructive evaluation, explosives detection, optoelectronic materials, and spacecraft contamination. Dr. Morgan served eight years in the Maryland House of Delegates, serving on the Judiciary, Ethics, and

Commerce and Government Matters Committees. He received his Ph.D. in Materials Science and Engineering from Johns Hopkins University in 1990; his B.S. in Physics is from Loyola College in Maryland.

DR. SAMUEL MUSA

Dr. Samuel Musa is a Senior Research Fellow at the Center for Technology and National Security Policy. Previously, he was Associate Vice President for Strategic Initiatives and Professor of Electrical and Computer Engineering at Northwestern University (1999–2005). From 1995 to 1999, he was Executive Director, Center for Display Technology and Manufacturing, University of Michigan. Prior to that, he was Corporate Vice President for Research and Advanced Technology, E-Systems (1983–1995). From 1979 to 1983, he served as Staff Specialist and then Deputy Director, Military Systems Technology, in the Office of Undersecretary of Defense for Research and Engineering. He was also Deputy Director for C3 Policy and Requirements Review in OSD (1978–1979). He served as Project Leader and Research Staff Member at the Institute for Defense Analyses (1971–1978). Also, he was Assistant Professor of Electrical Engineering at the University of Pennsylvania (1967–1971). Dr. Musa served on the Defense Intelligence Advisory Board, Army Science Board, Air Force Scientific Advisory Board, Air Force Foreign Technology Division Advisory Board, Air Force Logistics Command Scientific Advisory Board, and was Executive Secretary of Defense Science Board Summer Studies and Task Forces, and member of Scientific and Technical Intelligence Committee of the Director of Central Intelligence. He was a member of the Board of Directors of Semiconductor Research Corporation, Chairman of Aerospace Industries Association Technical and Operations Council, Member of Editorial Advisory Board of Journal of Electronic Defense, Technical Editor on Environmental Monitoring of IEEE Transactions on Geoscience and Remote Sensing, and Co-chair of Association of Old Crows Technical Symposia. Dr. Musa received Decoration for Exceptional Civilian Service from the Secretary of the Air Force, Certificate of Appreciation from Secretary of Defense, Certificate of Commendation from Society of Information Displays. He is a Fellow of the IEEE, Member of Sigma Xi, Tau Beta Pi, and Pi Mu Epsilon. He has published and presented over 85 papers in scientific journals and technical meetings. Dr. Musa received B.A. and B.S. degrees in Electrical Engineering from Rutgers University, and M.S. and Ph.D. degrees in Applied Physics from Harvard University.

MR. ROBERT PERITO

Robert M. Perito directs USIP's Initiative on Security Sector Governance under the Centers of Innovation. He is also a senior program officer in the Center for Post-Conflict Peace and Stability Operations where he directs the Haiti and the Peacekeeping Lessons Learned Projects. Perito came to USIP in 2001 as a senior fellow in the Jennings Randolph Fellowship program. Before joining the Institute, he was a Foreign Service officer with the U.S. Department of State, retiring with the rank of minister-counselor. He served as deputy executive secretary of the National Security Council (1988–1989). He was a congressional fellow in 1980. Perito received a Presidential Meritorious Service Award in 1990 for leading the U.S. delegation in the Angola peace talks. Perito served as deputy director of the International Criminal Investigative Training Assistance Program at the U.S. Department of Justice, which trained police in international peace operations (1995–2001). As a Peace Corps Volunteer, Perito served as a rural development officer in Nigeria (1965–1967). Perito has taught at Princeton, American, and George Mason universities. He holds a B.A. in international relations from Denver University and an M.A. in peace operations policy from George Mason University. Perito is the author of *Where is the Lone Ranger When We Need Him? America's Search for a Post Conflict Security Force*; *The American Experience with Police in Peace Operations*; and co-author of *Police in War: Fighting Insurgency, Terrorism and Violent Crime*.

DR. JAMES SCHEAR

Dr. James A. Schear was appointed as Deputy Assistant Secretary of Defense (Partnership Strategy and Stability Operations) on April 27, 2009. A member of the policy team in the Office of the Assistant Secretary of Defense (Special Operations/Low-Intensity Conflict and Interdependent Capabilities), Dr. Schear advises the Department's leadership on all matters pertaining to stabilization and reconstruction operations, foreign disaster relief, humanitarian assistance, international peacekeeping efforts and non-combatant evacuations. He also oversees the Department's efforts to assist foreign partners in their efforts to bolster stability within regions threatened by conflict or extremist violence. Prior to assuming his current duties, Dr. Schear served as Director of Research at the National Defense University's Institute for National Strategic Studies (INSS). He directed the Institute's analytic work in the areas of regional studies, national security strategy, defense planning, strategic concept development, and counter-terrorism/transnational threats. From 1997–2001, Dr. Schear served as Deputy Assistant Secretary of Defense for Peacekeeping and Humanitarian Affairs. In November 1999, he received the Secretary of Defense Medal for

Outstanding Public Service for his efforts during the Kosovo crisis. A widely published scholar in the fields of international security and conflict management, Dr. Schear has held research appointments at Harvard University, the Brookings Institution, the Carnegie Endowment for International Peace, the International Institute for Strategic Studies, and the Stimson Center. From 1984–1987, he served as Executive Officer of the Aspen Strategy Group. During 1991, he assisted the United Nations Secretariat in planning for the implementation of the Gulf War ceasefire resolutions, and he served as an advisor to the leadership of UN missions in Cambodia and former Yugoslavia from 1992–1995. During 2007, he served as a principal member of the Afghanistan Study Group co-chaired by General James L. Jones (USMC, ret.) and Ambassador Thomas R. Pickering. Dr. Schear earned his Ph.D. at the London School of Economics and Political Science. He also holds an M.A. from Johns Hopkins University's School of Advanced International Studies and a B.A. from American University's School of International Service.

About the Editors

SAMUEL MUSA is a Senior Research Fellow in the Center for Technology and National Security Policy (CTNSP) at the National Defense University. He has held the Homeland Security Science and Technology Chair at CTNSP. He has served in various positions in academia, government, and industry, including Northwestern University, University of Michigan, University of Pennsylvania, Office of the Secretary of Defense, Institute for Defense Analysis, and Office of the Secretary of Defense. Dr. Musa served on the Defense Intelligence Advisory Board, Army Science Board, and Air Force Scientific Advisory Board, and was Executive Secretary of the Defense Science Board Summer Studies and Task Forces, and a member of the Scientific and Technical Intelligence Committee of the Director of Central Intelligence. He is the author and co-author of several articles in scientific journals and technical meetings recently dealing with Counter Radicalization, Application of Law Enforcement Technology to Human Terrain Mapping and Counterinsurgency, Biometrics, and Risk-Informed Decision-Making. Dr. Musa received his B.A. and B.S. degrees in Electrical Engineering from Rutgers University, and his M.S. and Ph.D. degrees in Applied Physics from Harvard University.

JOHN MORGAN is the Chief Scientist at the U.S. Special Operations Command. He has served as the Deputy Director for Science and Technology at the Counter-Terrorism Technical Support Office (CTTSO) of the Department of Defense. At CTTSO, Dr. Morgan provides scientific advice to advance the work of the Technical Support Working Group and other activities to support the combating terrorism community. He was on assignment from the Department of Justice, where he directs the Office of Science and Technology, which is responsible for development of new technology for use in law enforcement. Dr. Morgan served eight years in the Maryland House of Delegates, serving on the Judiciary, Ethics, and Commerce and Government Matters Committees. He received a B.S. degree in Physics from Loyola College, and a Ph.D. in Materials Science and Engineering from Johns Hopkins University.

MATT KEEGAN is a Visiting Fellow at CTNSP. He is also Selex Galileo, Inc.'s (Selex) Chief of Staff and Vice President. He has written articles, case studies, and white papers on a range of national security topics ranging from technology application for counterinsurgency, Pentagon procurement issues, defense market direction, and strategic planning in the post–Cold War world. Mr. Keegan is a distinguished graduate of the National Defense University's Industrial College of the Armed Forces. Mr. Keegan has a B.A.

in Political Science from Syracuse University's Maxwell School and an
M.S. degree from National Defense University's Industrial College of the
Armed Forces.

www.ingramcontent.com/pod-product-compliance
Lightning Source LLC
Chambersburg PA
CBHW052111090426
42741CB00009B/1772